RETIREMENT GUIDE
FOR CANADIANS

RETIREMENT GUIDE FOR CANADIANS

An overall plan for a comfortable future

Henry S. Hunnisett

Self-Counsel Press
(a division of)
International Self-Counsel Press Ltd.
Canada   U.S.A.

Printed in Canada

First edition: March, 1975
Tenth edition: September, 1989
Eleventh edition: September, 1991
Twelfth edition: June, 1993

Hunnisett, Henry S., 1914-
     Retirement guide for Canadians
     (Self-counsel retirement series)
     ISBN 0-88908-288-X
1. Retirement — Canada. 2. Retirement income —
Canada. I. Title. II. Series.
HQ 1064.C2H86   1993   646.7'9'0971   C93-091184-9

Self-Counsel Press
(a division of)
International Self-Counsel Press Ltd.
Head and Editorial Office
1481 Charlotte Road
North Vancouver, British Columbia V7J 1H1

U.S. Address
1704 N. State Street
Bellingham, Washington   98225

*In memory of Norma,
my wife for 50 years: a beautiful woman,
a devoted helpmate, a loving wife and mother,
and my dearest friend.*

CONTENTS

PREFACE   xvii

1   ARE YOU READY TO RETIRE?   1

   a.   Two basic changes   2

   b.   A new life cycle   3

   c.   Accepting change   4

   d.   Are you ready for leisure?   5

   e.   The choice is yours   6

   f.   The test   7

   g.   Early retirement   10

2   THE PSYCHOLOGICAL REACTION TO RETIREMENT   12

   a.   The shock of job withdrawal   12

   b.   Lost goals   15

   c.   Alone in the dark   15

   d.   Variety — the spice of life   16

   e.   Financial concerns   17

   f.   On the bottom? Take the upturn!   17

3   FOR YOUR HAPPINESS AND PEACE OF MIND   19

   a.   Identify your problems and act   19

   b.   Is retirement justified?   20

	c. Financial security	21
	d. Attitude	22
	e. The importance of interests and activities	22
	f. Religion	23
	g. Choose new goals	23
	h. The promised solutions	24
4	CHOOSE FROM A SMORGASBORD OF ACTIVITIES	26
	a. Social activities	27
	b. Join the club	28
	c. Physical fitness	29
	d. Sports	30
	e. Entertainment	37
	f. Hobbies	38
	g. Continuing education	40
	h. Libraries and reading	42
	i. Politics	43
	j. Creative activities	44
	k. Travel	45
	l. Volunteer work	48
	m. New Horizons Program	51
	n. For self-starters	52

5 PERSONAL AND FAMILY RELATIONSHIPS IN RETIREMENT   54

    a.   Replace employment contacts   54

    b.   The strains of retirement on marriage   55

    c.   Your family   59

    d.   Family relationships   60

    e.   You become the receiver   61

    f.   Grandchildren   61

    g.   Sons- or daughters-in-law   62

    h.   Friends, old and new   63

6 THE SINGLE PERSON   64

    a.   The opportunities   65

    b.   To love and be loved   66

    c.   Should you marry?   67

    d.   Living alone   68

    e.   Living a satisfactory life   69

7 MONEY MATTERS   70

    a.   Calculate your total joint income   71

    b.   Your income checklist   72

    c.   How do you spend your income?   75

    d.   The final list   83

8 ESTIMATING RETIREMENT INCOME   86

   a. Important birthdays   86

   b. Checklist for income sources   88

   c. The Old Age Security Pension   89

   d. The Guaranteed Income Supplement (GIS)   93

   e. International agreements
      for foreign pensions   94

   f. Provincial assistance   95

   g. Provincial plans   96

   h. The Canada Pension Plan   96

   i. The Quebec Pension Plan   102

   j. Moving from one plan to the other   102

   k. Private or industrial pension plans   104

   l. Investment and other income   105

   m. Preliminary estimate of retirement income   106

9 YOUR COST OF LIVING IN RETIREMENT   108

   a. Income tax responsibilities   108

   b. Do not let them lapse!   109

   c. Your home   110

   d. Eating for health and pleasure   110

   e. Clothing   112

   f. Entertainment   112

   g. Vacations and travel   112

   h. Eliminate instalment payments   113

i. Medical and dental 113

j. Transportation 114

k. Bank charges 115

l. Evaluate each expenditure again 116

10 HOW TO INCREASE YOUR RETIREMENT INCOME 118

a. Part-time employment 118

b. Make your assets earn more income 122

c. Banking facilities 124

d. A prearranged instant loan 128

e. How to make your life insurance produce income now 129

f. Should you live on capital? 137

g. Annuities 138

h. Art objects and antiques 142

i. Your house or cottage 142

j. What should you do? 145

11 COPING WITH INFLATION 149

a. The squeeze — rising living costs, lower income 149

b. Investment and budgeting strategies to counter inflation 150

c. Government acceptance of responsibility 151

d. Government payment of certain expenses 151

xi

e. How the Old Age Security, Canada, and
Quebec Pensions increase   152

f. Your part in handling
changing interest rates   153

g. Which income may decrease?   154

h. Investments   155

i. Locking in current rates   156

j. Mutual funds   157

k. Real estate   159

l. Art, jewels, antiques, coins, and stamps   160

m. "The hedge"   161

**12 THE REGISTERED RETIREMENT SAVINGS
PLAN AND REGISTERED RETIREMENT
INCOME FUND**   163

a. The Registered Retirement Savings Plan   163

b. The final plan   175

13 PUT YOUR AFFAIRS IN ORDER   180

a. Legal matters   180

b. Funeral plans — the unpopular topic   183

c. Think of your spouse!   186

14 CHOOSING YOUR RETIREMENT HOME   193

a. What should it provide?   193

b. What should it cost?   195

c. Evaluating a retirement home   195

d. Making the choice   197

e.	Condominiums	200
f.	Co-operative apartments	207
g.	Rental apartments	207
h.	Mobile or manufactured homes	208
i.	The final move — a residence with medical and nursing services available	213
j.	Caring for an elderly relative or spouse	218
15	**WHERE WILL YOU LIVE?**	**220**
a.	Different views of moving	220
b.	Financial considerations	221
c.	Possibility of employment	222
d.	Should you stay near your old job?	223
e.	Milder Canadian areas	223
f.	Move to a foreign country with caution!	224
g.	Health	227
h.	Proximity to family and friends	228
i.	The retirement community	228
j.	Try it out first!	229
16	**YOUR HEALTH AND RETIREMENT**	**231**
a.	Find something to do	232
b.	Maintaining good health	233
c.	Enter the doctor	237

17 MAKING YOUR FINAL PLAN   241

  a. Set your goals   241

  b. The new value of time   242

  c. Do not believe it!   242

  d. Be active   243

  e. Love continues   244

  f. A life with quality   244

APPENDIXES

  1   Checklist for retiring   247

  2   Health care in Canada   251

  3   Canadian volunteer centres   253

SAMPLES

  #1 Gross income while employed   76

  #2 Estimated automobile expenses   84

  #3 How the money was spent   85

  #4 Estimate of retirement income   107

  #5 Estimated cost of living in retirement   117

  #6 Analysis of an actual insurance policy   135

  #7 Revising possible retirement income
      by rearranging assets   147

  #8 Maximum Canada Pension Plan survivor's
      benefits   188

TABLES

#1 Maximum monthly benefits under the
   Canada and Quebec Pension Plans   103

#2 Life expectancy   173

#3 Effect of income adjustments
   over 25-year period   179

PREFACE

a. WHAT WILL IT BRING?

The demands of the job have been left behind, the alarm clock has been sent to the Goodwill, and a steady stream of pension cheques, perhaps supplemented by additional sources, brings in a secure income. There is time to relax and soak up the sun in quiet contentment. It must be the ideal happy life, or so conventional wisdom would have you believe. But if you talk to a broad sample of retired people, a different picture emerges. Some, it is true, are very happy and they have never enjoyed themselves more. But many are unhappy and wish they could return to work and the life they knew during their working years.

Something has gone wrong. People who are released from their jobs at an age when they are still physically active and are provided with an income that enables them to live in comfort are supposed to have an automatic passport to happiness. Obviously this has not always been the experience.

b. WHY IS THIS?

Has there been a misunderstanding? Is more left behind with the job than is often realized? One day you have both a busy day and a day's pay: the next day you have neither.

This is a drastic change. There are questions to answer, decisions to make, and much to replace. Will your expected income enable you to maintain your present lifestyle? Will you be able to afford those new things which you hoped would put zest into your life?

Passing those hours spent at work in an enjoyable manner may be more difficult than expected, yet happiness may depend on it. There is no longer a superior to direct and help. You must recognize the problems and find the solutions yourself. Those who succeed usually enjoy life as much or more than ever. Those who fail are often bored, miserable, and resentful.

c. THREE REQUIREMENTS FOR HAPPINESS

At any stage of life there are three requirements for happiness: the first is sufficient income to support a satisfactory lifestyle, the second is to love and be loved, and the third is to feel that your life is being used in a manner that fulfils those needs and goals which you consider desirable.

The purpose of this guide is to eliminate guesswork and assist you to achieve this satisfying life. It clearly explains many of the financial benefits to which you may be entitled, some of which you may not be aware. Pitfalls are pointed out and solutions offered for avoiding them. How to determine housing needs and the possible advantages of retirement communities are discussed. Some of the ways others have found helpful in making a new and happy life are reviewed.

d. MARRIED OR SINGLE

Because most people who retire are married, and as retirement often puts new and serious strains on the husband/wife relationship, this topic is given extensive consideration in chapter 5. In this book, "you" refers to the couple unless the context indicates that it refers only to an individual. Further, recognizing that there is a growing number of women of retirement age in the work force, this guide is written to be applicable to both women and men. Both you and your spouse should read this text, no matter which of you is retiring, not only to help yourself, but also to assist you in understanding your partner's side of the change, and in recognizing when help is required and how it should be given.

As the number of single people, particularly women, who are retiring is increasing, there is a new enlarged section dealing with their situation as well.

Until recently, those who lived to an age at which they were no longer able to work and who had not saved enough to support themselves either lived in miserable poverty, or went to an institution that could provide little more than an existence, or they moved in with their families, often to be a burden on them. Now, in Canada and in much of the western world, there is genuine concern for the older person. This concern has been translated into a continuing stream of measures to give assistance and to make retirement an opportunity to enjoy a full and satisfying life. Chapters 7 to 12 discuss pension benefits and other financial concerns.

e. YOUR RESPONSIBILITIES

The key to a successful retirement is twofold. First, accept the idea that you can make this a happy time of your life, and, second, realize that you will have to work at it to make it so. *You can make a satisfactory life for yourself in your later years, but it is your own efforts that make it: society just provides the environment.* There will be many who fail to find satisfaction, some for lack of knowledge, others for lack of trying. Failure now can be the final disaster, success the crowning achievement of your life. Success will not only help you, but will take the strain of worry from your family and friends, enabling them to see you as a valued friend or family member. Your example will show what these years can be and will leave them with a cherished memory of you.

Note: The facts included in this book have been obtained from sources I believe to be reliable but they are not guaranteed. In view of the frequency with which changes occur, the reader is cautioned to use them only as a guideline for thought. Before taking action, you should check the facts to make sure they are accurate. This is especially so in matters of law or government policy, both of which are subject to frequent changes.

1
ARE YOU READY TO RETIRE?

Individuals differ in their expectations of retirement. Those who have found their work boring or stressful may think that leaving it will automatically create a better life. Others who have liked their work may fear that retirement will not be as enjoyable. Both may be unrealistic, for their views are based on an inaccurate understanding of the obligations and opportunities and what each person can and must do to create a new, different, and happy life. This could result in improper preparation and planning.

It is difficult to form an accurate mental picture of retirement before it arrives. All you have to relate to are your past experiences, and the closest thing to retirement is weekend and vacation time. But this is not a true standard for comparison, for a weekend provides a welcome break that is too short to get bored and is usually required for personal and family matters and necessary rest and recreation. Vacations are not fair standards either, for these are planned well ahead for concentrated pleasure that is often expensive and that you can afford, and often endure, for only short periods at well-spaced intervals. Retirement will be unlike either of these experiences.

Perhaps the best comparison can be made with a period of convalescence after an illness when an immediate return to work is forbidden. Even this is different because there was an end to it in sight. How did you find the time sitting around home? Were there things you could do indefinitely that you really wanted to do, or were you longing to get back to work? Did you ever consider what it would be like if you could never return to it again?

a. TWO BASIC CHANGES

Retirement inevitably brings two basic changes; both are deeply rooted and there are also other problems arising from them to be considered later. Success in creating a happy life will depend on your success in handling them.

First, the paycheque, that financial anchor of your working life, stops coming, which may cause an uneasy feeling. How much of it will be replaced by Old Age Security and income from other pensions, investment, and savings? Will you be able to live as you now do? If you are thinking of taking advantage of the opportunity to enjoy a new lifestyle, will you be able to afford it? There are things you can do to improve your income (chapter 10).

Second, your job has demanded a major part of your time and the best of your strength and energy. Its demands could not be refused. The next claim on your time was that which was required to service your home, prepare meals, shop, pay bills, and attend to other details. Only the remainder was yours in which to develop limited personal interests.

It may not be easy to stretch these interests to fill that great lump of time which was devoted to your employment. Surprisingly, to do so in an enjoyable manner is often the major difficulty in retirement.

b. A NEW LIFE CYCLE

An automatic washing machine performs by going through a series of distinct cycles: washing, rinsing, and spin-drying. When one cycle has finished, the next runs until it has completed its function and then is followed by its successor. Similarly, life begins with infancy and is followed by childhood, growth, education, and experiences in human relations. These are the necessary preparations for the next and longest cycle — your working life, during which you devote the best part of your day to employment in or outside the home.

The day you retire you end the lifestyle that began the day you started school, many years ago! During the intervening years, your schedule was generally set by others. As a child at school, you observed the routine laid down by the teacher, at home you followed your parents' rules. When you became an adult and acquired your own family and work responsibilities, more demands were put on you. Employment either provided for or contributed to, your support and that of your family and laid the financial base for retirement. You have given the best part of your life and strength to your work obligations. Now, on the day of your retirement, this cycle grinds to a halt. It is finished, period.

When the door closes after you for the last time on the day of retirement, your previous lifestyle will be left behind with the job. It will be filed away with the closed records of your past employment. You can't take it with you because that life was job-oriented and the job no longer exists for you. You are now on your own and must build a life completely different from that which you have been leading.

You have begun a new life cycle. You are released from the obligation of daily work and now have the right to use each and every day as you wish. It is a new game with a new team, played on a new field. Points are scored for making entirely new goals from those that previously counted. The rules are new but simple:

you and your spouse enjoy yourselves! Your joint interests are now in the forefront for the first time.

On the first morning there is silence; nothing will happen unless you make it happen. You have no demands on your time. There is nowhere you must go, no one you must obey, no job you must do to earn your income. This is the biggest change in retirement: *the control of time is now handed back to you, but with it comes a new responsibility, for you must learn to plan for its use yourself.*

c. ACCEPTING CHANGE

The next step in making satisfaction a reality is to accept that there must be a great many changes in your life. Any fears you have about retirement are really just paper tigers, much greater in imagination than reality. Once faced, they lack substance and fade away.

Everyone dislikes change. It means the loss of the familiar and the introduction of the unknown. However, the changes that come with retirement are different in one very important respect from those that were forced on you by work or other obligations. You may now choose those you will enjoy. Look on it as the means of release from the old bonds and an opportunity to build a new life according to your chosen plan.

Anticipating what time will mean after retirement is difficult. It is common to think that retirement will simply be an endless series of holidays; many people never think deeply enough about it beforehand to see the fallacy in this. When everyday becomes a holiday, the appeal is lost.

So it is with leisure time, when it becomes a twenty-four-hour-a-day, seven-days-a-week continuous life-time supply. Unless much of this leisure time is filled with activities of interest and some activities that include obligations requiring some effort, it becomes a boring, frustrating hell.

Think for a moment about time and how your value of it has changed over the years. As a young person, you probably considered it a renewable resource. If you made a mistake or failed in some endeavor, there was always time to try again. Your dreams were all still possible but, as the years went by, there were more candles on the birthday cake and certain things turned out to be final. Patterns unlikely to be reversible developed and limitations became evident. Time began to take on greater value. Frequently, events of a serious nature drive it home — the passing of friends and contemporaries, graying hair, illnesses, growing children.

The solution to this problem is easy to see, but more difficult to put into effect. Often you must work as hard at enjoying retirement as you did to earn your living. For some, the answer is to continue working and find another job. But most of us must face the reality that our retirement system is designed to get us *out* of the work force.

d. ARE YOU READY FOR LEISURE?

Before you are faced with imminent retirement, the thought of having unlimited time at your disposal probably seems like Utopia. However, unless you have prepared, when retirement arrives it may not be as delightful as you expected. You are so conditioned to working full days, generally against a time schedule, that subconsciously you will expect it to continue. For years you have strived to arrive on time, complete jobs on time, keep appointments, and do so much per hour. Regardless of what your job was, time was a steady master and you were the puppet on its strings.

Nice as it is to be released from this bondage, you may find yourself unprepared for leisure. Subconsciously, you may feel that there must be something you should be doing, somewhere you should be going, and you may feel guilty for having so much free time. The change is so sudden that it is difficult to relax and enjoy this new-found freedom.

There are no standard "rules" of how to best use your time. No two people are exactly alike; some require an almost frenzied schedule, even in retirement, while others will be fully satisfied with a rocking chair and slippers. This is the reason that it is continually emphasized throughout this book that you must suit *your* needs and build a program that fills *your* personal requirements.

e. THE CHOICE IS YOURS

Perhaps for the first time you and your spouse, if you have one, can be perfectly selfish. The responsibilities to your job and family have been fulfilled, and your only obligation is to yourselves, so start out to do all those things you have been unable to do for the lack of time.

Start by listing all the things you enjoy. There may be much icing here, but that is good, for you are entitled to it. Then think of other things your personality may require.

Others may attempt to influence your choice, feeling that you should enjoy the things they do. Consider their suggestions but make your own choices, for no one else can really know what will be of most value to you.

The daily activity of making your living has made a most important contribution to your life. Dr. Bronowski in *The Ascent of Man* states: "The most powerful drive in the ascent of man is his pleasure in his own skill. He loves to do what he does well, and having done it well, he loves to do it better."

You must replace this essential part of your life with something just as satisfying. You will want some continuing responsibility that you are obligated to perform (the word "obligated" is important) and some activity in which you are very involved as essential ingredients in a replacement for work.

f. THE TEST

To determine how well you are prepared, answer the following five questions carefully and honestly. Writing the answers helps in this respect, for in answering verbally, it is too easy to let it slip by with the observation, "I guess I know that."

It is advisable to make a list of things which you could not answer properly. Knowing what they are will make it simpler to recognize the answers as you read through this guide.

1. Am I in a financial position to live in a manner that will be satisfactory to me and my spouse?

You should first know your total present household income and what parts will continue or cease. You should know not only how this has been spent, but how the total has been divided among the major categories such as food, housing, medical, etc. You must also have an accurate estimate of your retirement income and to get this may require some investigation. Then, estimate what changes in expenses can be expected. Many of the expenditures listed above may continue, but there will be important changes.

Deducting any reduction and adding any anticipated increases will provide an estimated cost of living in retirement. Comparing the estimated expenditure with the income will indicate what your financial position will be; essential information to make a realistic retirement plan. Chapters 7 to 10 will provide detailed assistance in working out these matters.

2. Will I be able to use my time in a manner that will make life enjoyable?

How well you are prepared to use your time in a satisfactory manner is something in which many deceive themselves. There is a tendency to think that things will just automatically come along to occupy this new daily eight- or nine-hour stretch of time in an enjoyable manner, but that is unlikely to happen. A few interests occupying a short time each week is not enough. It is essential that you have interests and/or activities started which can be expanded to take up the slack. If not, you must add new activities to do so. How you succeed in handling this challenge may determine the quality of life in the coming years. Chapter 4 discusses the opportunities.

3. Am I mentally prepared to accept the change from a working life to retirement?

Everyone has a self image. Our society values work as a virtue. Your employment has been an important part of your image, both to yourself and others. You have lived up to this demand, paid your way, and have to feel that it has contributed to your worth and status. After retirement, some erroneously continue to use the working world's standards and by so

8

doing, see themselves as without further value. Some even give up and pass away.

It is essential that you realize that your past accomplishments cannot be taken away, and to also accept that that chapter is finished. There are now new standards of value in which paid employment is not included. This is not an easy transition, yet accepting it is necessary for contentment and peace of mind in retirement. These matters are investigated in chapter 3.

4. **Do my plans take into account the wishes, interests, and welfare of my spouse so that we will be able to live happily together?**

During the working years, many of the decisions affecting all aspects of life were dictated by employment and were accepted by both spouses. After retirement, with those demands gone, each spouse may desire to fill the void with things of personal interest but which may not be enjoyed by the other partner. Each should understand the other's needs and wishes and be willing to compromise when necessary to maintain harmony. This is considered in chapter 5.

5. **Will my present home help or hinder my life in retirement? Are there good reasons to remain, or to go elsewhere?**

Your home and its location will play an important part in every aspect of life. Those things that were important when working and raising a family may be disadvantages after retirement. Its suitability should be seriously considered. The following questions must be answered (see chapters 14 and 15):

- Will it be too expensive?

- Will its location enable you to reach those interests you desire?

- Is it convenient for family and friends to visit?

- Will it be a source of satisfaction?

- Would a home designed and located specifically for retirement be a better source of new interests for you?

g. EARLY RETIREMENT

The number of persons taking early retirement is increasing. Obviously, they expect that it will lead to a better life. For this to be realized, there must be sufficient income to support the new life they seek. Observation reveals that the majority have correctly assessed their financial positions and are free of money problems.

There is a second requirement, and in this, many have not been successful. Those who retire for a specific reason, to get into a business or occupation which they believe will provide a much better life or to carry out a well-prepared, fulfilling plan for their lives are usually happy. But others, who retire just to escape the job without a plan to replace it with a better life, not realizing that this could be dull and unhappy, often wish that they had remained where they were.

Leaving a job at or near retirement time is usually an irrevocable step. Your decision will be a personal one and should be made only after a careful understanding of what the step will mean, and how you and your spouse will find life if you take that step.

If you wish to take early retirement, make a realistic assessment of your position using the questions listed above. If this reveals that you are not ready, there are options. Remain employed until your preparations are completed, try to work out job improvements with your employer, find a better job, or grin and bear it until you are ready. There should be many more years of life, but it is your responsibility to make them happy ones. Spending a little time in preparation may be the key. It will be well worth the effort.

2
THE PSYCHOLOGICAL REACTION TO RETIREMENT

A group of retired people with whom I was working filled out a questionnaire that was designed to reveal how they were enjoying retirement. Twenty-two of the twenty-five indicated difficulty in accepting and enjoying their new-found leisure because they were plagued by thoughts that something was "wrong." There was no reason why they should have these thoughts, but they did, and the thoughts would not disappear by simply being told to go away. Unwarranted fears can monopolize your thinking, become absorbing obsessions, and make your life miserable. Retirement is a fertile seedbed for this problem.

This chapter considers some common causes of this condition. Once the causes are understood, it is possible to see the solution.

a. THE SHOCK OF JOB WITHDRAWAL

The change from long-term, full-time employment to retirement is too great for most people to experience without suffering some kind of reaction. How serious your reaction is depends on three things: the satisfaction you derived from your job, the preparation you have made for retirement, and your ability to cope with a change of this magnitude.

The reaction can range from a simple feeling of being lost, uprooted, unwanted, bewildered, and alone in a strange world to breakdown and mental illness which, fortunately, is uncommon.

1. Loss of the familiar

Everyone experiences difficulty when faced with the loss of the familiar. The more important and long-standing the subject the more difficult the transition. Consequently, the loss of your long-term employment will rate high on the problem scale; the daily routine has been torn away leaving a great gap.

The years of repetition wore deep grooves and your life slipped along easily in them without the need for guidance; it will be difficult to change direction. You must now learn to chart your own course, which may require persistance.

The job was the hinge on which your life was hung; it determined which way that hinge could swing and what could be permitted in the time remaining after working hours. You couldn't accept anything that would place your job in jeopardy, particularly as you grew older and jobs became more difficult to find. Your strength was used to fill the job's demands, and only the surplus was available for personal purposes. Your home was located to be accessible to your job and your family could be uprooted and moved to a new location when the job required it. It was your "security blanket" and you are bound to feel insecure without it.

2. Loss of job satisfaction

The satisfaction a job provides is not usually appreciated until it is gone. Often, the paycheque is considered to be the main source of satisfaction, yet if you lose your job, it soon becomes apparent that there is much more to employment than money alone.

13

This may comes as a surprise, especially if you considered your job as difficult or unpleasant and longed to be able to give it up. Only after you do so is it obvious that the strain and the annoyances that provided mental activity in themselves are certainly preferable to boredom.

Retirement takes the pleasure of work from you; now it is essential to find alternative sources of satisfaction. It does not seem reasonable that there should be so much difficulty once you are given this opportunity, but there is. Your mind has been living with a comfortable pattern, the road familiar, the direction clear. This is wiped out, and, just at the time when unclouded thought and effort is required to set the new direction, the shock of it all seems to confuse and stop all motion.

3. Loss of identity

People identify with their jobs; they think of themselves as machinists, accountants, executives, teachers, etc. Your job identity is an important part of the mental image you have of yourself. By retirement you may have accumulated seniority or risen to a position of importance that earns deference and respect from others.

Before retirement, these things are of real value to any individual who enjoys them. But after retirement, all these will vanish! It is a shock to realize that the attributes that were considered personally yours, and which were the reasons for your importance, have been taken away and given to your successor. You stand outside the door; inside the work goes on as before, but without your help. You are no longer needed, nor are you the person you thought you were and that important identity has been lost. You may be bewildered, unsure of who you are or what you should be doing.

14

b. LOST GOALS

The feeling that you have a purpose in life with a particular goal to reach is essential to a fulfilled life. Part of life's goal for a working person is usually the attainment of some position in the future; for a homemaker it is a well-run home and the achievement of a plan for the children.

Doing your job and raising your family have been the main goals that supplied purpose to life. Now, both those goals have been reached and you may be left feeling that there is no longer any reason to continue. It is a depressing thought, and the empty days may come and go with no apparent reason for their existence.

The feeling of guilt that is so prevalent in the early years of retirement is another manifestation of the same background. You, like most people, have probably been taught that you must work to live and, if you don't, you aren't pulling your weight. This thought can well up and gnaw at your peace of mind.

c. ALONE IN THE DARK

One of the basic human pleasures and needs is companionship. Often, a job provides this as the people you work with become good friends. In addition, your workmates provide many other benefits: they will discuss your problems with you and provide support when troubles come; they do not hesitate to bring you back into line when you are off the beam or are worrying unnecessarily; if you develop a swelled head, they cut you down to size. All this will be missed and may contribute to a feeling of loneliness, one of the most deeply felt problems of older people.

A group of men discussing changes that retirement had brought to their lives agreed they had experienced a very noticeable and unexpected difference in the attitude of their old business friends. When they left work, they had realized and accepted that they would not be welcome back, but had expected their colleagues to continue their friendships. They felt that these friendships were built on mutual enjoyment of each other's company, and it was a shock to find that they quickly faded after retirement. In fact, the friendships arose from proximity and their value in the work place; once these no longer existed, new friendships took their places.

There is another aspect more difficult to understand: those still working tend to consider a retired person to be as much an outsider as someone who has quit and gone to work for a competitor. Perhaps this change of attitude is due to an understanding that retired people must develop a new lifestyle, for they have stepped into another world.

d. VARIETY — THE SPICE OF LIFE

After a day at work, returning home is anticipated with pleasure. But spending all your time at home can be boring. After a demanding but absorbing daily routine, a succession of empty days can be devastating.

The job's roots spread out in many directions, thereby contacting and bringing back nourishment from many sources. When there is nothing to take the place of the daily trip to work, it is too easy just to stay at home, all day and all night, and this frequently happens. Nothing can contribute more toward boredom.

During your working years, you are forced into the mainstream of life by job and family, but now it is easy to avoid involvement. The stream is still flowing and, while you need not venture out into the rapids, there are many suitable areas, calmer but wonderful, waiting to be discovered. Get out and recapture the variety.

e. FINANCIAL CONCERNS

A steady job provides security with its paycheque; haven't you known since you started that you must work to live? It is difficult to make your subconscious mind believe otherwise. Will the income from social security, pensions, and other sources be safe? Will my income be adequate? Will inflation continue and will it lead to financial problems?

While no one knows what will happen in the future, there are some practical steps you can take to secure yourself financially in retirement. Again, planning is the key. (See chapters 7 through 12.)

f. ON THE BOTTOM? TAKE THE UPTURN!

There is good reason to be apprehensive about retirement, but it doesn't mean that part of your life need be an empty and frustrating experience. Retirement is a personal experience and each person's will be his or her own, different from that of everyone else. If you observe those who retired a few months ago, there will be little uniformity; their feelings will be as different as their faces.

At one end of the spectrum are those who have prepared and, while they may have experienced some unexpected reactions, on the whole they are getting along well. At the opposite end are those who were completely unaware of what was coming; they are unpleasantly surprised and many of them will be among those who promptly sink into oblivion.

Most people, however, are between these two scenarios. They probably expected life to be something like

17

it was on weekends and vacations, so the actual experience is a shock. "Retirement shock" has become a common phrase, with good reason. People who experience it are bewildered and drifting. They have no goal or purpose; they want something to fill the void, yet know neither what it is, nor where to find it. Their rank, status, and identity have gone; they are unrecognized and unnecessary. But it may be just the darkest hour before dawn; there is no way to go but up, and it is up to you to change direction.

You don't have to make the turn unassisted. If you are scraping the bottom, now is the time to assess your attitude and make up your mind that this is enough, that you *will* take the future in hand and find the way to enjoy the rest of your life. Read on for some helpful ideas to get you started.

3
FOR YOUR HAPPINESS
AND PEACE OF MIND

a. IDENTIFY YOUR PROBLEMS AND ACT

Among the major problems you may face are unhappiness and boredom. Identify the problems, and then understand and tackle them. Some problems may be handled by simply understanding, rationalizing, and putting them in perspective to reduce them from their imagined to their real size.

If action is required, take it at once, for delay only causes unnecessary worry. Do what you can, then stop worrying. Try to concentrate on something else, preferably something enjoyable. Undesirable thoughts tend to lose their strength and fade away if they aren't called upon. Another ally is time — the great healer — for its passing dulls the sting and allows solutions to take shape.

Once a problem is identified, you may not be able to solve it in one step, but often a partial solution leads to another. Do as much as you can, then accept the final reality and resolve to live with it. Do not permit it to ruin your life. In the case of those changes that you just do not like, such as the loss of importance, remember, THERE IS NO REAL PROBLEM. THE DISTRESS IS CAUSED ONLY BY THE WAY IN WHICH YOU ARE REACTING TO IT.

It is perfectly normal to have such feelings, and they are not easy to chase away, but keep in mind that it is

19

only your *reaction* that is causing the problem. Most of the psychological problems are without real substance and, if put in perspective, disappear. If some are real and persist, don't despair, there are solutions for them all.

b. IS RETIREMENT JUSTIFIED?

You may be feeling bitter about having to retire, or even about choosing to retire if things have turned out differently than you imagined. To evaluate fairly whether or not retirement is justified, you must review the period through which you have come and see how major events have formed the opinions by which you live.

The world was very different when you were young. There was very little security, the "work ethic" was unquestioned, and pensions and retirement were not expected. You probably didn't think about voluntary retirement and it was sprung on you too late in your life to permit your ready acceptance of it. You probably expected to work until old age forced a stop, well past 65.

Many feel that retirement is a direct statement that they are too old to be of further use, not just in the job but in anything. They believe they no longer have a valid reason to continue. That might be so if the sole purpose of life is to put in a full day at the same employment until forced to halt. But who decreed that? Until recently, even in the western world, the supply of the necessities of life was limited, and it was not possible in any country to do anything else but wring the last ounce of work out of everyone. Retirement could not be universal.

The advent of the automobile, truck, and tractor and the mechanical, chemical, and computer revolutions made possible increased production, so that since the turn of the century, hours of work have been greatly reduced. No one feels guilty about that.

My grandfather used to speak of an acquaintance who worked in the steel mills in Pittsburgh about one hundred years ago; the steelmaker's shift was twelve hours a day, six days a week, with one twenty-four hour shift ending each two-week period. This was followed by two days off to prepare the way to change from day to night shift, or vice versa.

The great increase in productivity since that time has also made retirement for everyone at a specific age feasible. You have done your share; with widespread unemployment, your work is no longer required, so retirement need bring no feeling of guilt.

Government at all levels has made this obvious by providing pensions and many medical, hospital, and other important benefits either free or available at a greatly reduced cost. Private organizations offer discounts or other advantages. The people, through their elected representatives, indicate their wish to support and expand these programs. It is obvious that these steps are proof of society's wish to offer them as a reward for a job well done.

c. FINANCIAL SECURITY

Your income is probably more secure now than it was during your working life. You could have been fired, become ill or injured, necessitating either employment at a lower income or, perhaps, even unemployment with limited income from a disability pension. Your particular skill might have been eliminated by progress.

Continued employment depended on many things, but your retirement income is secure with no strings attached. Your government pensions are certain and indexed against inflation. Indeed, almost any contractual pension is also safe. There are many sources of aid open to you, and any retired person having financial problems should start by inquiring at the local municipal level. If the problem is beyond their power, you will be directed to the proper source.

d. ATTITUDE

Your attitude will play a most important part in determining if you will have a happy retirement. It is a controlling factor in morale, and high morale is sought by every competitor, organization, business, or team. It is recognized as an essential ingredient in becoming a winner in any field, and it contributes heavily to satisfaction and happiness.

High morale is based on the confidence that you can and will succeed. It can provide the strength to enable you to reach out and try new and often difficult things, or to put up with an inconvenience to enjoy something which you might otherwise pass by. It can impart an enthusiasm for life.

e. THE IMPORTANCE OF INTERESTS AND ACTIVITIES

It is common for those who enter retirement unprepared to fail to see the necessity of keeping busy with satisfying pursuits. Activity can make life worthwhile, especially if you sincerely enjoy it.

An example of this is the story of a widow in her seventies who showed symptoms of a common complaint of older people — arthritis. This woman did not complain about her discomforts and seemed quite happy. Inquiry revealed that, a few years after the death of her husband, she had decided to take up dancing, which she continued to do as often as three times a week. It not only kept her mobile, but brought her into contact with others. She thoroughly enjoyed and looked forward to these outings, and this provided the incentive to ignore and rise above the conditions that might otherwise have depressed her into a state of self-pity and inactivity.

f. RELIGION

There is another factor of major importance which may affect serenity or peace of mind. I know of no race or tribe ever discovered, regardless of how isolated its location, that did not have strong beliefs in some system of gods or a superior power that controlled the world and those who live in it. For centuries, a strong religious faith has provided peace of mind for many and those who possess this treasure are fortunate to have the solace it brings.

In recent years, the discoveries of science have weakened the tenets of religions, and have undermined their acceptance by many. People who have experienced this are left in a vacuum that is waiting to be filled. While this situation is not caused by retirement, as you grow older it is common to question the purpose of your life and whether or not there is a "hereafter." Unanswered questions may become stumbling blocks to your peace of mind.

After retirement, many of those persons who have drifted away find comfort in returning to their religious roots.

g. CHOOSE NEW GOALS

Everyone needs a goal that provides the feeling that something worthwhile will be accomplished by its achievement. The difference now is that the value of these things is not measured in hours spent on the job or the size of the paycheque, but in human terms not so easily evaluated.

Your obligations are now the care and enjoyment of you, your spouse, your children, and your grandchildren; participation in the lives of your peers; and perhaps volunteer work in the community. These things may be more important than the work you did over the preceding years, which was motivated to provide income. Now your efforts are directed by other human values, a goal just as or more important than the previous one.

You are free to decide what you wish to do. Do not expect to be without problems, but realize that they can be overcome and that the solutions to them can be very satisfying.

h. THE PROMISED SOLUTIONS

At the beginning of this chapter, solutions were promised. They are clear and simple:

(a) Identify and understand your problems.

(b) Put them in proper perspective.

(c) Take any necessary action to solve them.

(d) Find activities that will satisfy your personal requirements.

(e) Set up new goals with your spouse to provide a purpose for your lives and a direction for your energy. The satisfaction derived from their pursuit and achievement can make an important contribution to your happiness and peace of mind.

Retirement is, for many, one of the happiest stages of life. Some even take it early so they can start enjoying the life they always wanted. It can be that way for you, too, but only if you make it so.

4
CHOOSE FROM A SMORGASBORD
OF ACTIVITIES

The morning you step out into the new world of retirement is like starting down the line at a smorgasbord with an empty plate. There is an appealing variety of dishes — some will please you, some will not. You are free to take your pick, fill your plate, and then come back for more. If you try something new, but do not enjoy it, you are not forced to eat it. There will be more than you can possibly sample, and there just will not be room for everything.

Any activities that you enjoy now can be the base on which to build a plan for your retirement. You may have hobbies and activities you want to continue to pursue. The problem is that they probably won't fill this great new expanse of time. You can take extra training to improve your skill or knowledge and broaden your scope, but this may still not be sufficient.

If you find yourself with time on your hands, there is a wide choice of activities available. You must select those that appeal to you and then take the initiative to enjoy them. Even if you are restricted by cost or physical disability, there is still plenty to choose from. It is amazing how content many people with severe handicaps often are; most of them adjust to their disabilities and build happy lives. Although they must miss many activities, they find satisfactory alternatives.

If you are forced into unwanted retirement and feel that nothing can take the place of your job, change that thinking now. Once into these enjoyable activities, you will, like so many others, wish that you could have retired earlier! People who are bored have only themselves to blame for refusing to try new things. For your own sake as well as for those around you, be a sport and try!

In this chapter, there is a broad range of activities to suit any kind of person: those who are active or inactive, those who are happiest in a group, or those who are loners.

Make up a mix that will provide the most satisfaction and that will cover all seasons. It is best to include some with obligations to a schedule to get you out of the house. Be sure to have a variety in order to avoid boredom.

a. SOCIAL ACTIVITIES

You may need to find new friends and social activities to take the place of those associated with employment. There are many opportunities, but you must find them and make the effort to participate. Many groups such as religious and municipal organizations stage seniors' events, often for a specific purpose such as exercise groups, dinners, or card games.

Card games are perhaps the most widely enjoyed seniors' social activity, as almost everyone plays. Being able to play opens up a whole new area, for card players are always seeking others to participate. Playing cards may bring more invitations to join others than any other contact. If you do not play, you will miss much of the social scene; have a friend teach you or take lessons.

Card-playing has another desirable feature, for if you are on vacation and staying in a hotel or trailer, you need only invite someone to play and, suddenly, other vacationers who were previous strangers become friends.

Sharing a meal with friends either at home or in a restaurant is an enjoyable social event. For many, it is their only social activity.

b. JOIN THE CLUB

A helpful move is to join a senior citizens' club. Established groups are located in almost every place of worship, regardless of the denomination. These are usually service groups organized to benefit anyone who wants to join; you don't have to be a member of the particular religious group to participate. As well, the YMCA, YWCA, YMHA, some municipalities, and other interested organizations also sponsor seniors' groups.

If there are several clubs available near your home, talk to some of the members of each before joining. You would be well advised to spend some time at each to ensure you choose the one with the most compatible membership and activities you enjoy. If there is no group near you, get together with a few others and start your own.

Many organizations offer special treatment and rates for seniors that are often not well advertised. Often there are activities, trips, or vacation plans offered that you might not otherwise hear about.

You will find new friends who can introduce you to the retired way of life and who will replace many of your friends who are still working and have less free time. You will be welcome in the group; most are looking for more members, for the larger the group, the easier it is to get enough people to stage special events.

The great value of joining a seniors' group is, first, that its members will have interests similar to your own and, second, there will be many people who will be a source of assistance and information to advise you of opportunities of particular interest to senior citizens.

In addition, group members organize many interesting activities. You name it, some group somewhere probably does it. Choose a club with people with similar backgrounds, interests, and means: their plans will probably please you. Suitable entertainment for your group may be a bus trip to the country in the autumn to enjoy the colors or to a nearby city to see a show or to shop. The possibilities are endless.

c. PHYSICAL FITNESS

There is a widespread acceptance of the value of physical fitness for bodily and mental health. Those who do participate not only often find it a most enjoyable, beneficial, and absorbing activity, but claim that they look and feel better. As a bonus, it may make possible participation in more physically demanding activities, often to a greater age. Make sure you have a medical examination to determine your body's safe limits of exertion.

A useful book regarding health and physical fitness is *Fit After Fifty*, published by Self-Counsel Press.

To be effective, a regular program is needed which can be chosen from many options, depending on what you enjoy and how much effort you wish to put into it. Walking and swimming can be the least demanding, but the effort can be increased if desired.

Regular periods of calisthenics, those exercises which you may have learned at school or in the services, may suffice. These may be supplemented with simple equipment such as weights or spring-loaded devices requiring greater exertion. Workout rooms with more sophisticated equipment are often available at community centres, public and private clubs, apartment complexes, and retirement communities.

Sports are part of maintaining physical fitness and participating has additional advantages. It helps give the feeling of being part of the active world, makes you feel younger, and gets you out of the home and in contact with others, all things of importance at this stage.

d. SPORTS

There are many sports suitable for older people; some are enjoyed by men and women in their eighties. Some sports are for the individual, others require a team. Some are strenuous, others are not.

Summer is the easiest time to enjoy sports, but winter offers many opportunities too, so when building your list, make a point of finding a variety of things to do in all seasons.

1. Curling

After retirement, you are likely to find most team sports too strenuous for your participation. There is one notable exception, made to order for Canadian winters — curling. Facilities are available nearly everywhere.

Curling is the ideal sport for retired men and women because it is readily available, need not be expensive, and can be practiced either by team members in a competitive schedule or by occasional players participating as desired.

Young people work hard at the sweeping part of the game, but older groups generally leave it for the individual to decide how hard he or she wants to work. Many people curl into their eighties and even some with physical disabilities are able to participate. There is no real work in throwing the stone; it is simply raised from the ice, swung slowly as a pendulum, and released to allow its weight to carry it along on the smooth ice.

Everyone is welcome. There is a place on each team for the inexperienced player as the "lead." Leads are often in short supply and the more experienced players expect and welcome them.

The real aim of the game at this stage of life is social, so there is no pressure to win as there is in younger leagues. There are times available for men's and women's games as well as mixed games in which you can participate with your spouse. Start at any age; someone will be glad to teach you.

An added bonus is the number of people you will meet. There are eight people in every game and you will meet other teams as well as you play through a season.

To the newcomer, the courtesy shown to all in curling and the desire to make the game a pleasant experience is very noticeable. Curling is a game with no referees and no one is expected to "make" every shot. Everyone is welcome except a complainer.

Do not hesitate to try curling. You will probably have friends who play, or you can look up the local arenas and ask for information. There is almost certainly a nearby group that will welcome you.

2. Swimming

Swimming in the ocean, in lakes, or in swimming pools is one of the most enjoyable experiences of childhood.

31

As an adult, your obligations may have left you little time for swimming, but now these obligations have gone. It is still as much fun as ever, and in addition, it offers many health benefits. Swimming is a complete exercise — you use every muscle. Also, immersion in water has a therapeutic effect because it takes your mind off other things.

There may be suitable local waters but pools are the main source for retired people. There are indoor public and private pools which are open year round, and almost every retirement facility has one. If you don't know how to swim, don't let that get in your way; you can learn. Many pools have staff who give lessons to adults. Many also have exercise programs which take place in the water. The buoyancy of the water can assist those with muscular problems to exercise.

3. Skiing

While not everyone will be able to ski after retirement, two developments in recent years have broadened the opportunities for participation for seniors.

First, modern chair lifts and tows make the ascent to the top of the hill or mountain pleasant, and groomed trails make downhill skiing easier. Hills are graded and marked with the degree of skill and effort required, so you may select the easier slopes or those within your ability.

Second, the popularity of cross-country skiing has opened new vistas. Cross-country skiing is less expensive and there is little danger of serious accident. It simply involves trekking through the country on skis and is mostly done on trails that have been cleared. You can make it as physically challenging as you want; there may be hills, but usually the trails avoid steep slopes.

Provided you are not too cocky in the appraisal of your skill, you can select a suitable trail, enjoy the outing, and come back to the starting point still on your skis, not on a stretcher. It is a very pleasing thing to see older people skiing on a bright winter day, doing it their way and enjoying themselves as much as the younger ones. Equipment is usually available for rent if you wish to try it out.

4. Golf

Summer provides the opportunity for a much broader range of sports, one of the most popular being golf. There are courses of all kinds, varying in degrees of physical effort required, expense, and skill.

One of the recent developments is the "executive" or "par-three" course. These courses are much shorter with holes running about half the length of those on a regular course. They are generally less challenging, and they fill the need for those who lack the skill and stamina to handle 18 full-length holes. It is made to order for the non-expert retired couple and enables them to have a pleasant game.

Power carts can be rented at most courses, which help reduce the physical effort required. Choose the course that best suits you.

Another advantage of taking up golf is that it is available everywhere you go. It can be a real interest on a southern winter holiday. You can learn at any age. If you regard it as a pleasant outdoor experience, rather than a challenge to become an expert, you can learn to play well enough. Courses are not crowded in the off hours during weekdays and you will be welcome as a learner at that time. Join a club or "pay as you play." It need not be expensive.

5. Snowmobiling

Snowmobiling is another sport suitable for your participation. This activity has mushroomed rapidly and gained widespread acceptance. Snowmobiles can travel through snowbound winter woods and make cottages not previously accessible in winter useable throughout the year.

There are both public and private areas with cut and groomed trails and machines available for rental. The snowmobile has made it possible for many to get out and enjoy the Canadian winter scenery.

6. Fishing

Fishing has always fascinated both men and women as it contains elements of gambling, surprise, and mystery. It is, after all, one of the rare sources of a free lunch. To many, "the catch" is the goal, but even more important is the opportunity it affords to enjoy the peace, quiet, and beauty of the outdoors.

Anglers' clubs or associations exist in most areas. Fees are minimal and joining one may be a good source of information and instruction if required, as well as a pool from which to draw new companions.

Summer, with its better weather and open water, is the usual season for fishing, but it is a sport that may be enjoyed all year. Ice fishing is very popular now that improved facilities are available. Snowmobiles and tracked vehicles have made safe transportation to more distant spots a routine operation. You need not have your own vehicle, as transportation is often provided to the rental fish huts.

Now that you have the time, you will be surprised to find how many places there are for reasonably good fishing, even in or near very crowded cities. Spend some time around the available water and ask questions at the marinas and tackle stores to learn about renting tackle and to get directions and advice. By starting this way, you will know better what to buy if you decide to continue with the sport.

7. Walking and hiking

Don't neglect walking as a combined form of sport, physical activity, and an interesting way to pass the time. Walking is an activity that your doctor will probably recommend, but to be of value, it should be done at a suitable rate and for a long enough distance.

If you tire of walking the same routes, try some variety. Go to new parts of the city or country. Most people who have lived in an area have not seen its points of interest, the ones that the sightseeing tours visit. Why not plan your walks to cover accessible districts of possible interest? You may be surprised to discover new and fascinating haunts.

Clubs and other organizations often plan walks to interest people in wildlife or bird watching. These walks are usually advertised to the public. Why not go at least once to see if you enjoy it?

8. Hunting

Many people have often wished to participate in hunting but never had the time. Now, for you, this is no obstacle. To find a group, inquire among friends. More women are participating in hunting and equipment manufacturers are producing suitable items for them.

Join an association of anglers and hunters, go to the meetings, and meet new friends and contacts. Or, join a gun club; most groups need new members from time to time and you don't need to be an expert shot. Don't hesitate to participate.

You may enjoy local hunting near your home either by yourself or with a group of friends. If you don't know the regulations for your area, call a sporting goods store or ask at the local anglers' or hunters' association. There you can find information on seasons, open and closed areas, and licence requirements.

There is a progression of open seasons that make it an annual sport. Autumn is usually a busy time for hunting big game and migrating and local game birds. Winter is the rabbit and hare season, and spring and summer are good for hunting pests like crows, ground-hogs, prairie dogs, or other nuisances, depending where you live.

Hunting has the advantage of providing a purpose to visiting the country and enjoying it. The scenery, fresh air, and activity, which can be as strenuous or limited as you wish, provides a welcome change for many from city life.

9. Boating

Boating is possible almost anywhere there is water. If you don't own a boat, start by renting and see if your interest develops. It is best to have some experienced person accompany you in the beginning as there are many possible hazards with which the uninitiated may not be familiar.

There are many types of boats ranging from skiffs, punts, and canoes for those who wish to propel them-selves, to power boats with small outboard motors, to yachts. Sailing has a fascination of its own and there is usually at least one sailing club on any water large enough to support it.

Many people find that boating opens a new world of interest for them. A craft with living accommodation may take the place of a cottage, or in warmer climes may provide a winter vacation.

10. Bowling

Indoor bowling is popular with both men and women and is a combination of sport, exercise, and social event. It is most actively pursued by clubs formed by work groups, churches, senior citizens' organizations, or other associations. Teams are formed and they play and compete on a regular schedule.

Don't neglect an opportunity to participate for it can be a fine interest all year round. Most bowling alleys have reserved times for leagues as well as open times when the general public can play. This provides an opportunity to go on a prearranged outing or on the spur of the moment as a couple, a family, or with a group of friends.

e. ENTERTAINMENT

Entertainment will have a new place in your life now that you have much more time and the freedom to spend it in this very enjoyable way. You are free to choose the time when the entertainment is most readily available and the prices are lowest. For example, many organizations have special discounts for seniors but they are restricted to certain times of the day or week. Don't hesitate to ask if special rates are available wherever you go.

Some theatre chains issue special identifying cards that you must show to purchase the ticket at a discount. Inquire at your local theatre for more information. They will tell you what proof of age is required and give you your identification application. You can usually get even larger discounts if you attend a function as a member with an organization or group. A chartered bus, for example, may reduce the transportation cost and add to the fun.

Look into the available opportunities. Read the advertisements and, above all, ask your other retired friends. Most of them take great pride in being a source of information and are very pleased to be asked for it.

f. HOBBIES

There are many hobbies of absorbing interest and that continually demand that you expand in skill, knowledge, and technology. You might want to pursue your hobby for personal pleasure only or work at it seriously with a definite goal in mind — perhaps to meet acceptable commercial standards and sell your product.

Most boards of education, community colleges, and technical schools offer inexpensive classes that may fill your needs. Private lessons will cost more, but may be necessary if you want to develop a really professional finish. In some areas there are privately run trade schools that aim to develop a commercial standard of skill in a trade in which employment is available.

It may be an advantage to strive for saleable results from your hobby. You will have a goal and be forced to improve, practise, and keep at it. This will assist in overcoming the lethargy and loss of interest that can so easily come to the retired person who is no longer subject to the demands and discipline of a job. Selling your work can also give that sense of achievement and success that may otherwise be lacking in your life.

Some hobbies, such as those described below, have almost unending possibilities and are usually accompanied by membership in a very active club or group that can provide opportunities for an expanding circle of friends and social activities.

1. Carpentry

You might try your hand at building furniture, boats, cupboards, or an addition to your cabin. Some people enjoy making models or furniture from kits, others from more complex plans requiring considerable skill. If you have no experience and you need training, look into courses at your local community or technical school. Once you learn how to measure, cut, join, smooth, and nail, you have the rudiments to do almost anything. Your early efforts may be rough, but with practice and a serious interest, you can become proficient.

Most libraries have many books showing the structural methods used in making anything from a doghouse to a violin. You can also learn about furniture refinishing and other carpentry techniques.

2. Gardening

If you think of gardening as simply planting, watering, weeding, and watching things grow, think again. That is only the beginning to what can be an exciting hobby.

If you are interested, you can read up on those plants that interest you and become an expert. You may then go on to plant breeding and even the development of new strains. The hobby opens the way to flower shows, clubs, and new friends with similar interests.

You don't even need a big space; apartment balcony gardens are common. In some locations, you can rent small garden plots, and, if you grow vegetables, you can help deflect rising food costs.

Gardening need not stop with the end of summer. Indoor gardening under lights can let you enjoy your hobby year round. A greenhouse can be relatively inexpensive, but even that is not necessary. Fluorescent lights permit the establishment of a garden in the basement at practically no cost. You may grow winter blooms or have your plants started indoors and ready to transplant when spring arrives.

3. Photography

Everyone enjoys looking at pictures. Taking a good photograph requires skill as well as luck, and it involves an understanding of composition, lighting, and timing.

This hobby can be pursued with an inexpensive camera or can be expanded as far as your interest desires and your finances permit. Camera clubs are everywhere. Their members will welcome you and be most willing to teach you new techniques. You might find you even move on to developing your own negatives and printing your own pictures.

4. Bird watching

As well as finding and observing birds, it can be fascinating to study identifying marks, record normal seasonal migration dates, and look for unusual species.

This interest, again, can lead to new friends through shared interest and club membership. Local clubs often gather annual migration records and public participation is invited in seasonal "watches."

A bird feeder in your garden can keep you busy observing all year. You should also buy a good bird book and a pair of binoculars to assist you in identifying new species.

g. CONTINUING EDUCATION

If you have thought of continuing your education, now is the time. In recent years there has been a broadening of opportunities, range of programs offered, and entrance requirements.

There are basically two classifications. The first is the study of more serious disciplines, often with the aim of attaining a degree. If you wish to attain high school or university graduation status, you can often do this through a local institution or by correspondence. University degrees, in particular, have become more readily available in this way. Some courses provide, in addition to written material, tape recordings and the opportunity to phone your professor long distance, at no cost to you. Entrance requirements have also been reduced or eliminated for the "mature student." It is not necessary for you to work for a degree or standing; attendance can be simply for your pleasure.

I had the pleasure of sitting on a panel on a TV show in Vancouver with a gentleman who stated that he had never had any formal education. At the age of 68 he was accepted at Simon Fraser University where entrance requirements (other than a six-month provincial residence rule) are waived and tuition is free for mature students. He simply selected the courses he wished to take, attended the lectures, and read further on them in the library. He was not required to write examinations or meet standards. Attendance was simply for his own betterment and pleasure and he was thoroughly enjoying the experience.

The second classification includes those subjects that lead to the development of skills that you want to pursue simply for interest or that may be saleable. A growing number of institutions offer courses in subjects in the hobby field such as art, house repairs, gourmet cooking, and acting. They also teach a large number of commercial subjects.

If you want part-time employment, you may find that a course will either provide new skills for you or bring rusty ones up to saleable standards. You may take such a course in the evening while you are still working in order to be ready for retirement, or it may be best for you to take it as a full-time activity after you have stopped working.

You might also want to look into part-time employment in the field of continuing education. Many school boards now employ retired persons as part-time teachers for instructing children, tutoring those requiring extra attention, and conducting language classes for newcomers. Teaching qualifications are not usually required. If interested, enquire at your local board.

h. LIBRARIES AND READING

You may find a hobby that has no cost. A fine example of this is reading, perhaps the most widely pursued interest of the retired. It can be expensive if you buy all the books and magazines you would like to read, but a good alternative is using the public library. It is full of interesting reading, instructive titles, and current magazines. You can read them there or take them home. Many very interesting hours can be spent in this manner even if you only look at the pictures! It is an interest to be enjoyed when desired — and you should have as many of these interests as possible to fill in otherwise blank days.

If you walk into a library with no object in mind and simply look around, read titles, and thumb through pictorials, you will almost certainly find yourself taking down one or more books or magazines and becoming interested. It will be surprising if it doesn't result in your taking books home and you may find yourself starting to read much more, or having a new interest in a hobby you read about but had never considered before. If you don't use a library regularly, visit one and let nature take its course!

i. POLITICS

Everyone should be interested in politics and government; they are the basis of democracy. Federal and provincial members have "riding" associations that remain active between elections. Most locally elected people also have some organization where much of the work is done by volunteers.

Choose a candidate or something you wish to support and turn up at the meeting. Join the organization and offer to help. You will be welcome; this is just what is needed and can develop into a real interest for you.

At election time, there is often paid work within the association or at polling booths. Such jobs, of course, go to the faithful who were there ahead of time. Don't ignore this activity if you have an interest in the government at any level. It will also help to keep the views and needs of retired people before the politicians. People over 65 form a steadily increasing percentage of the population. This is a very important voting block and receives attention from all levels of government, but to be effective requests must be made by organizations that represent a number of people. An individual carries little weight with a politician. There are organizations, such as "Pensioners Concerned" whose purpose is to promote the views of seniors and aim for government support. Your participation is needed and will be welcome, so join any such organization available in your district that advances ideas you consider desirable.

j. CREATIVE ACTIVITIES

Some people are creative by nature and must use this gift to feel fulfilled. If you have such an interest, there are groups of people available almost everywhere who help each other or there may be an instructor. Many school boards have night school classes that can lead to more serious study involving private lessons.

Once you become involved in art, you discover a whole new world. You see things so much more clearly and appreciate the real beauty. An art gallery takes on a new interest and a quick trip through one is no longer enough. You can spend a whole day studying one painting! Local exhibitions become an event to watch for.

If you are creative, try different things until you find the application that interests you. It may be clay modelling, painting, carving, or whatever; any interest becomes fascinating and engrossing once you get into it.

Most people feel that they must have inborn talent to do creative work, but this is not so. A school teacher specializing in art tells me that 90% of painting is learned and only 10% is natural talent. This means that almost anyone who is interested in and enjoys this creative hobby can learn to paint well enough to achieve satisfying results. Instruction and then practice are the basic requirements.

If you are going to enjoy painting, practice will be most interesting as you see your skill improve with each picture. If you are interested, don't be afraid to try.

k. TRAVEL

1. Take advantage of discounts

If you want to travel in your retirement, either to sight-see or to avoid the long winters, take advantage of special rates available to seniors. Off-season and group plans are often surprisingly low. Some are genuine bargains, for many organizations charge seniors a lower price for the same service. Others may just reflect low quality. Speak with someone who has taken the same tour to determine if it will please you.

Wherever you wish to go — to the local museum, Florida, or to see the Great Buddha in Japan — you should be able to find "package tours." These have many advantages, more so now that you are older and can use the extra help. The cost is usually fixed and your baggage, hotels, transportation and, sometimes, meals, are all looked after for you. You will probably find compatible companions in the group and there is always someone responsible if you need assistance, making it more comfortable for a single person to travel.

Ask air, bus, and rail lines about fares, package plans, etc. Travel agents often have specials; look around, it is surprising what is available. Don't give up because you think the expense will be too great; there are many low-cost package tours, charter flights, and group plans. You may be pleasantly surprised that you can afford many memorable trips. Some are now planned specifically for seniors.

2. Elderhostel Canada

Elderhostel programs provide a unique, inexpensive way to travel and see new parts of the country. You will travel with other like-minded men and women, 60 years of age or better, and attend lectures about a subject that interests you. There will be ample free time to explore and enjoy the country around you. A few programs even allow children and grandchildren to come along.

Most Elderhostel programs are one week in length. Programs begin on a Sunday afternoon and end the next Saturday morning. During your week you will be offered three courses which meet every weekday for about one and a half hours. While you are only required to attend one course, the courses are scheduled so that you can take all three.

The Elderhostel philosophy is "simple accommodations at modest cost," so the dormitories and other host institutions where you'll be staying are not like hotels and other commercial facilities. Usually there are two twin beds per room and single accommodations may also be available. Bathroom facilities are generally shared.

While Elderhostelers are usually favorably impressed by the generally high quality of institutional food, it is intended to be wholesome and nutritious, but not fancy or up to gourmet standards.

Each Elderhostel host chooses the courses it wants to offer, anything from nature studies, history, and geography, to art and hobbies. Elderhostel courses are given in every province and territory and cost about $295. You must provide your own transportation. There are also international programs in Greece, Italy, and Mexico at a greater cost. For more information and a catalogue contact

ELDERHOSTEL Canada
33 Prince Arthur Avenue
Suite 300
Toronto, Ontario M5R 1B2

3. The trailer and the recreational vehicle

Those who like to travel, to get on the road and roll along to new places, to meet new people, to follow the seasons, have found these vehicles to be the ideal means of fulfilling these wishes. You can become as mobile as a bird, free to roam the continent and experience the life of different areas.

These are two different kinds of equipment. The trailer is towed behind a car or light truck. It ranges from a simple, ingeniously designed box on two wheels which opens up to provide the platform for a tent, to a much larger, more luxurious vehicle.

The recreational vehicle (RV) is a self-propelled, bus-like vehicle with its own motor. Both the larger trailers and the RVs are equipped with toilets, kitchens, sinks, stoves, refrigerators, and beds. They are in reality, small, mobile apartments. Most people find the facilities for living quite adequate and easy to use and maintain. They are compact homes that accompany you to provide a familiar, inexpensive dwelling, and you avoid the inconvenience of packing and unpacking. They also provide the camaraderie of trailer park life, usually places where friends are more readily made than in motels or hotels.

Living in this manner introduces you to a new way of life. Sometimes it is the only home, but more often it becomes the travelling home that is used to go south in the winter, north in the summer, and often anywhere else you fancy in between. Stay in one place as long as you wish, move when you desire. There are trailer camps almost everywhere, some in public parks, others privately operated. Most have sewage, power, and water hookups. Central buildings often provide supplies and recreational, laundry, and shower facilities. People who enjoy this type of life are inclined to be friendly and quickly make contact with each day's new neighbors. Those who enjoy each other's company often form groups that travel together or that meet at prearranged destinations.

For many, retirement brings the opportunity to indulge in this kind of life for the first time. It has numerous advantages, the most important of which is the way in which it can lift you out of a rut and provide a new and exciting lifestyle. The contact with different people and the opportunity to try new things and see different areas can stimulate and revitalize your life and outlook. Many people have found it to be the means of building a fascinating life in retirement.

If the RV lifestyle appeals to you, it is a simple thing to investigate. Go to nearby trailer camps; the people there will be happy to talk to you. Visit dealers to see the different types of RVs. At first, you would be wise to rent different units for short trips so you can find out if you do enjoy this lifestyle and, if so, exactly what features you prefer when you decide to purchase a unit.

(For more information, see *Mobile Retirement Handbook*, another title in the Self-Counsel Series.)

1. VOLUNTEER WORK

Shakespeare once wrote, "Mercy...is twice blest, it blesseth him that gives and him that takes." (*Merchant of Venice*, Act IV, Scene 1)

The same can be said of volunteer work. There is a tremendous need for people willing to give assistance to the disadvantaged. If you have time to give and a desire to help, there is plenty of scope. It would be impossible to list all the things that are done by volunteers, but the range is broad.

You need to consider your own personality before you volunteer. Some people find it too difficult to work with people with certain disabilities or who live in difficult situations. But the choice of activities is so broad that you should be able to find something suitable.

If you don't know where to begin, ask any religious leader for suggestions. Try the YMCA, the Community Chest office, or the Red Cross. Many cities have a volunteer centre to advise those wishing to do volunteer work of available opportunities, so inquire and locate an opportunity suitable for you.

There are volunteer centres in every province and all of them are looking for volunteers. The variety of opportunities is great and changes with the area. Volunteers are needed to work in the following fields:

With children — social services, teaching, tutoring, leisure time activities, and day care

With the elderly and handicapped — visiting, delivering meals, craft work, shopping, telephoning

Service to immigrants — information, teaching, social outreach

Hospitals — visiting, crafts, shopping escort, etc.

Mental health — distress centres, telephone counselling, crafts, group involvement

Corrections — a friend to one on probation or parole

1. Canadian Executive Services Overseas (CESO)

CESO is a non-profit corporation operated by a group of Canadian business leaders with the support of the Canadian government. Its main objective is to assist developing countries achieve economic growth by helping them strengthen and improve the effectiveness of their own organizations and institutions. (There is also a specific Canadian Indian program to help native peoples with economic, social, and local government development.) CESO receives requests from developing countries for the help of experienced Canadians for specific tasks and then matches up the task with a volunteer capable of performing it. The possible openings are very broad including manufacturing, agriculture, training, engineering, merchandising, administration, health, mining, lumbering, finance, and transportation.

Volunteers may be presently employed or retired. They are not paid for the services, but CESO pays air fare for spouses when the assignment is two months or longer.

Serving such a term overseas has many benefits. There is the enjoyment of seeing another culture, being received as an important person, and the pleasure of passing on one's knowledge for the benefit of others. If these rewards are not enough, there is the expense saved by the provision of food, lodging, and entertainment, and the new status that you may be given on your return. Many will be interested in your experience and you may be sought out by organizations in the field to learn what is being done over there, by others as a speaker, and by friends who wish to hear about it. These factors will assist in building a sense of personal worth at a time when it is vitally needed. To apply, write —

CESO
Suite 2000, 415 Yonge Street
Toronto, Ontario
M5B 2E7
(416)596-2376

m. NEW HORIZONS PROGRAM

The New Horizons Program is a way of enabling retired people to create projects of their own choosing and to obtain the necessary money to set them in operation. If the application is approved, money may be supplied to pay expenses for a maximum period of 18 months. If necessary, an application can be made for an extension of an additional 18 months.

The basic aim of the program is to provide financial assistance to groups of retired people who have a suitable idea but lack funds.

The project should have at least 10 volunteers who will serve as directors of the project. The majority of the directors must be retired, and the management must be clearly in the hands of the retired members, although non-retired volunteers may be involved in and benefit from the project. It should enable retired people to use their talents and experience to help themselves and others and answer a community need. The project should aim at reaching out to as many retired people as possible.

Although the project is not designed as a money-making proposition for its participants, the New Horizon grants should be regarded as seed money, and the project should become either self-supporting or obtain funding elsewhere when the original grants terminate.

The federal Department of Health and Welfare, which oversees the program, reported that in the first 10 years they sponsored 20 213 programs with $124 836 901, which reached one-third of the retired population — some in every province and territory. The programs covered an extremely broad range of topics and included almost anything of value to make life easier or more enjoyable for those retired.

Activities fell under the following headings:

Service oriented — day care, meals on wheels, letter writing, driving, visiting

Historical — local research and recording senior citizens' organizations

Sports and fitness

Research and media — directories, cookbooks, arts and crafts, hobbies, and entertainment

If there is no local office near you, contact the national office:

New Horizons Program
Health and Welfare — Canada
6th Floor
Brooke Claxton Building, Tunney's Pasture
Ottawa, Ontario
K1A 1B5

n. FOR SELF-STARTERS

It has been estimated that about 10% of the population are leaders and the rest are followers. During working years, economic necessity and the urgings of parents and spouse force even the most shy person out to work. When that phase is over, many followers are inclined to remain at home rather than start out to build their new lives, and it is they who frequently give up, have difficulty in adjusting, or simply fade away.

Help may come from two sources. First, family and friends can provide the push to get them involved. Second, those who start activities for the retired and draw the followers in to participate also help.

Here are two things that those of you with leadership ability can do: first, invite your retired friends and any others that you can reach to join you in your activities; second, start things in which others can participate.

The opportunities are limitless. Take, for example, Mr. Wilson Abernathy, who started an organization known as Associated Senior Executives, a firm with a list of retired executives who have a wide range of experience, and who are available for temporary hire. This organization enables these executives to continue to use their experience and ability at a less strenuous rate and to earn some extra income. It also gives the businesses hiring them the benefit of their experience that would otherwise not have been available on a temporary basis or at as reasonable a cost.

5
PERSONAL AND FAMILY
RELATIONSHIPS IN RETIREMENT

In many ways, married and single people will have the same problems and opportunities after retirement and should, therefore, take the same steps to prepare for it. There are, however, basic differences that require separate consideration.

Those who are married will have the support of a spouse to fall back on, but will also have new problems injected into their relationship at that time. This will require mutual effort and understanding to avoid friction.

For single people, the replacement of job-related personal relationships may be one of their greatest priorities. To better understand both groups we shall look at the situation from the standpoint of married and single people separately and the contribution that family and friends can make to their lives after retirement.

Whether you are married or living alone, your relationships with those who care about you become more important. Loneliness is one of the most serious problems of older people. Love and friendship prevents or cures it, and the assistance of others, if not a necessity, can be a comfort.

a. REPLACE EMPLOYMENT CONTACTS

In chapter 2, the value of the contacts made with your fellow workers was discussed. In retirement all this is lost, for the break with your fellow employees is usually complete. You will find yourself forced out of their circle and kept out by the walls within which they work. It is difficult to maintain their friendships, and, even if you do, they cannot fill your new needs during the working day when you want friends to help use this new-found time. Their spare time may be used for chores and family matters, and they may have little time for you. You will be alone in a strange and unknown world. It may be a very startling shock and the contribution which these people made must be replaced for the sake of your health and happiness.

In addition to replacing these personal contacts, another need arises. As the years go by, your physical condition and strength deteriorates and the assistance of others in the simple matters of daily living may become of great importance. At some point you may be able to continue in your own home only with help; without it, it may be necessary to enter an institution where help is available.

Expanding relationships to provide love, friendship, and support becomes one of the basic needs in these years. Knowing you are accepted by others and have friends is important to your self-esteem. Once your job is gone, you need people to keep you in contact with the world outside yourself and to help you avoid becoming too dependent on your spouse or family.

b. THE STRAINS OF RETIREMENT ON MARRIAGE

There are major changes in retirement, which, if not amicably solved, can cause a breakdown in your relationship and perhaps in your marriage. This is unfortunate, for retirement is a time when husband and wife will be spending more time together and will be increasingly dependent on each other for companionship and assistance.

There will be change, but the important thing is to use the change well and understand what is happening. Use it as an opportunity to make this a new and enjoyable stage in your partnership.

Before your retirement you both had pleasant days on your own and evenings you enjoyed together. There were things to tell each other and the variety of contributions brought from your separate days made your time together enjoyable.

Think of the change! Being together all the time can be boring. You experience the same things. There is nothing new to discuss. Both may have lost outside interests. Such a situation may spoil the most valuable thing any married person can have at this time: a happy spouse and a happy home.

No one would knowingly cause this kind of problem. There is no need to, provided you understand that there may be serious repercussions and that you make the effort to avoid them.

1. A wife's independent life

Many women are at home when their husbands retire. If they were employed, they probably retired at an earlier age, and if they remained at home to raise a family the children have usually moved on. Women who have been at home have been free to plan as they wish and have made independent and enjoyable lives of their own. This may have included a hobby, volunteer, social and/or recreational activities, and time spent with friends. They may have chosen to work full- or part-time. This took place during the work day so their husbands were not involved. These personal and separate lives were a definite part of their identities, as important to them as jobs were to their husbands.

Their lives were much more than housekeeping and shopping, which they may continue after their husbands retire. In this respect women often never retire, and men mistakenly assume that this is their wife's only life. Men may think that to be around home to keep their wives company will not change things and will perhaps make the days more interesting. This may not be the way the women see it.

2. Who will be in charge?

Housework and shopping may be a source of friction. After one or both of you retire, the division of labor will change. The problem is that each of you may have very different ideas of how it should be done, and both of you may attempt to assert your standards and methods and try to take over as the boss.

You need to sit down and redefine your roles. If one of you has been responsible for most of the housework in the past, then the other should ask where the most help can be given. You might want to list the tasks and assign duties.

3. Don't spoil it!

Studies reveal that retiring men often find it more difficult to adjust than women. Women may be more adaptable, have a greater interest in their homes, and have more social activities than their husbands. Unless the man is able to develop independent interests, he may be frightened and concerned about the future. He needs someone to help him and the obvious person is his spouse, the only one who has any deep personal interest in him. He may find himself following her around the house, expecting constant attention. If you fall into this trap, you are reducing your spouse to the position of a personal servant.

This is a most unfair and one-sided attitude. It is not a solution, for not only does it provide nothing of interest for either spouse, but it may spoil the relationship making both unhappy and resentful.

Many wives who have stayed at home feel that the husband has worked all his life, often under considerable pressure, and now this is his time. She does not understand what he needs or can do, and therefore hesitates to interfere, and tries to help by staying at home with him. This is neither a fair nor effective solution. It is up to both to take the initiative and find activities and interests of their own.

Discuss the future and work out a mutually acceptable plan. Accept each other as equal partners. While working, the demands of the job were paramount, but this is no longer true. Now is your opportunity to do those things together that you have wanted to do but which were not previously possible. At the same time, you may both keep many of your independent interests. To achieve this, decide what you wish to do together, what is most important to each one individually, and work out a schedule to allocate the time to make them fit together.

4. Both can benefit

The best decisions are usually made in an atmosphere of trust and goodwill, the worst when one of the participants feels that the other wants to dominate and get an unfair share. Selfishness in the demands made by either person without considering the wishes of the other could cause feelings of animosity or of "being used," making a mutually satisfactory solution impossible. By granting your spouse's most important wishes and

showing a willingness to compromise, you set a concil-
iatory tone and may receive the same treatment in
return.

Professionals who help couples with marital problems often state that the solutions are frequently found
in improving attitudes. They refer to the way in which
courting couples act. Each person emphasizes his or her
good qualities and suppresses those which may not
please. They are courteous and considerate; selfishness
is restrained. The whole relationship is directed toward
harmony and mutual enjoyment of the time together.

This behavior is easier under the spell of new love
and romance. After many years of marriage, courtesy
and consideration may be forgotten. Professionals sug-
gest that it is possible to reintroduce romance into a
mature marriage, which can inject a spark of real pleasure and interest into your life. Try it. In this atmosphere, it is likely that a solution bringing the greatest
benefit to both parties can be achieved.

Full personal development arising from respect for
each other's individuality and desires, coupled with the
benefits and close companionship of marriage, can do
much to achieve the second requirement for happiness
— to love and be loved.

c. YOUR FAMILY

The main source of friendship and/or love and support
comes from your family. It is a rare person who does
not have some relatives. The more distant relationships
that might be ignored by those who have a large family
and children of their own can be of utmost importance
to those who have not. Even those now single may have
children from a previous marriage. Whatever your position, cherish your relatives and strengthen the connections.

The family is constantly changing as new members enter by birth or marriage, and as those within it grow through the successive stages of life. A three-generation family may be a self-contained and self-regenerating unit. There are children to enjoy, mature people to help them, and younger adults to assist the older members. As you grow older many of these changes are to your advantage.

The importance of the family relationship may not be entirely recognized prior to retirement because it has not yet fully developed. Your own life may not have arrived at the point where the need is apparent or the contribution you can make is appreciated. Its importance is obvious if you discuss it with and observe those living in retirement. Grandchildren and family are the most important topic of conversation. Many who move away from them to fill other interests soon find that nothing takes their place and often move back to be near them. You may be appreciated as a sitter, to look after the children, to give parents time for other things. Do not avoid this, for it is one of the connections that binds a family together.

d. FAMILY RELATIONSHIPS

In the past, three or more generations of a family frequently lived together. Under the circumstances that then existed, particularly on farms, it could work well. Everyone's help was needed, there was more living space, the hours of work were longer, there was less leisure time in which friction could occur, and parents were accorded greater respect. This situation may still exist in rural settings or where the parent is pleasant, flexible, and everyone loves and enjoys each other. There are also some cultures that place greater importance on family solidarity than others. When close family life works, it can be a fine solution. More often, however, it is not a happy arrangement, and other solutions where each generation lives separately but in contact, is frequently preferable.

e. YOU BECOME THE RECEIVER

The stage of your life in which you constantly gave has turned into another where you may become the receiver. If you have children, they are by now probably on their own. That period in which their actions may have placed a strain on your relations and thrown up barriers between you has ended. They could not learn from your experience but had to do so from their own. The crash landings and the burnt fingers from which you could not save them not only served to break the apron strings, but also matured them and may have restored you to your rightful position as their most valuable friend and ally. No other relationship can be as trustworthy, loving, and secure.

As they become more firmly established financially, they no longer need your support. If they have a family of their own they mature, recognize, and now appreciate what you have done for them. They were once dependent on you but the relationship reverses and as the years go on you may need and rely on their help.

f. GRANDCHILDREN

A new and most pleasing aspect enters with the arrival of grandchildren. Their full value cannot be explained, it must be experienced. It is a natural instinct to continue the race, and their presence assures it during your lifetime. They bring back your younger years. We all love children, but these are not ordinary children: they are your grandchildren. If you show interest they return it with unfeigned and enthusiastic love. Who would not respond and feel flattered when a child so obviously enjoys your company?

You will be wanted, for this is an opportunity to give as well as receive. You have a contribution to make to both children and grandchildren and they may learn much from you. The young ones will observe you going through the final stage of the life cycle and will pick up knowledge to use in preparation for their later years. You can teach them your values. More may be taken in and stored away for future use than is realized at the time. You are in an enviable position when compared with their parents, for not being responsible for discipline means you can concentrate on enjoying them. It makes a difference that often enables grandparents to maintain a hold on their grandchildren and to reach them when they are breaking away from and perhaps ignoring their parents.

g. SONS- OR DAUGHTERS-IN-LAW

The family expansion brings a possible problem, for the marriage of your child introduces a stranger into a key position. This new son- or daughter-in-law can decide to welcome or reject you, and that decision may be made in response to your treatment and how you accepted him or her as a spouse for your son or daughter or if you have attempted to interfere with their lives. It will obviously be an advantage to have a warm and friendly relationship with your in-law if you are to see and enjoy each other with any frequency.

Avoid complaining, for listening to it is no pleasure. They will recognize your problems; it is not necessary to continually talk about them. Keep your proper place; raising their children is their responsibility, not yours. You had your turn. To interfere may make you most unwelcome. Visits will be more enjoyable and frequent if they are made for the pleasure they bring, rather than grudgingly as a duty that must be performed.

About one of three marriages now break down, which introduces a disruption at the family's heart. Feelings can run high, sides may be taken, and one group may have little to do with the other. If this situation exists, it may tear at your peace of mind. If any grandchildren are in the custody of the one with whom you are not on good terms, there may be difficulty in seeing them. Not only will you miss them, but they may be scarred by bitterness that can affect them the rest of their lives. These unfortunate side effects can be lessened if you are able to keep an open mind and remain on good terms with both partners. By so doing, the personal hurt to both you and your family will be lessened and the benefits you derive from the relationships, and those which you contribute, are more likely to continue.

h. FRIENDS, OLD AND NEW

The second main source of support comes from friends. There is a depth of comfort, feeling, and understanding between old friends that takes years to grow and it is desirable to turn to them first. The newly available time makes it possible to spend more of it with them and perhaps re-open connections that may have been interrupted by the demands of raising a family or earning a living. You are a fortunate person if there are enough friends to fill your needs.

If not, turn to other retired men and women, for they are in the same position and are looking for new friends too. The problem in the larger cities is to find and meet those who have interests similar to your own. To do so, you must go out and visit those places where they may be found.

6
THE SINGLE PERSON

As a single person, you have the same needs as someone who is married. You need enough secure income to live in an acceptable manner, to love and be loved, and to be satisfied with the way in which you are spending your time.

About one-third of the population aged 65 to 70 is single. Over two-thirds of this group were once married but have lost their spouses through death or divorce. In the 70 and over age group, the proportion of singles rises to one-half, and this increases as the groups grow older. The majority of them have suffered one of the most severe shocks that can be experienced — the loss of their spouse — and their adjustment to retirement may be more difficult than for their married counterparts.

The basic difference between a married and single person at this time is that the single does not have the support of a spouse to provide a built-in companion and helpmate. The singles must find their new activities themselves. Friends may be sympathetic and try to include them in their activities, but singles just do not fit well. This loss of married friends and the kind of activities enjoyed by couples may be deeply felt.

It is unfortunate, but even for married couples, at some point, death will take one spouse and leave the other alone. This is not the end, and it is quite possible to make a new, satisfying, and meaningful life with others who are in the same position.

a. THE OPPORTUNITIES

The opportunities for enjoyment and fulfilment for older single people have broadened greatly in recent years. Business sees the proportion of young people in the population shrinking, and the number of older people expanding at the same time. They are, therefore, placing greater emphasis on filling new demands. All levels of government are trying to recognize and live up to their responsibilities. Retired people are asking for the things they want and are helping build the organizations to satisfy them.

A generation ago, many things were closed to women and they were welcome at others only when they were accompanied by their husbands. Now very little is denied them and they can enter on their own.

All these things, however, are like attractions set up at an amusement park or fair: they are there for your enjoyment, but you must act to buy the ticket and enter.

1. Organized activities

One of your greatest priorities may be making new social connections and finding new friends. There are many organizations to help: senior citizens' centres, churches, and religious and ethnic organizations, all of which often provide a meeting place where retired people with similar needs and interests can come together to fulfil them. They usually have permanent quarters, open daily. There is always something going on. There may be card games, crafts, courses of interest to the members, lunches, organized trips, and dances. Everyone is welcome regardless of marital status or sex. It is one place where men and women, single or otherwise, may be together and may help fill the desire of single people to mix with the opposite sex. The permanent staff are often able to help with problems or can

65

direct you to other more suitable sources. The members have a wealth of information about activities, discounts, and other useful facts.

The possibilities for fulfilment and happiness through the friendship and activities with others are very broad, so a single person need not spend a secluded, dull, or lonely life. Once again, all this is out there waiting; what you get is up to you.

2. Financial

The financial position of single retired people will vary widely. Those who have worked all their lives and never married could be in the best financial situation. At the other end of the scale, widows who never worked in paid employment are, as a group, in the worst financial position.

As retirement approaches, everyone, married or single, should take the same steps to understand what their financial situation will be and to make the best use of resources. Those who feel incapable of this task, perhaps because their now-departed spouse looked after this part of their affairs, should concentrate on learning how to do so, and/or seek the service of an accountant, trust company, or financial advisor. These financial matters are discussed in later chapters.

b. TO LOVE AND BE LOVED

People are individuals and needs vary widely. Some singles feel most comfortable in groups and draw strength and pleasure from numbers. Others must have privacy: to them, two is a crowd. They enjoy time alone and are not lonely. But even a loner requires love and support, and it becomes more essential as time goes on.

Most of us are somewhere in between. Your feelings in this matter will influence your relationship with family and friends, the home chosen, and the activities in which you participate. Determine what is best for you and make every effort to achieve it.

Love is a word with many shades of meaning. In blood relationships there is a difficult-to-define element that cannot be shared with others outside the family. It is real, you are born to it, and it cannot be surrendered. It is the source of the deepest values in marriage.

There can be a deep affectionate attachment between friends that is also a form of love. More often this relationship is simply friendship, a less intense feeling of pleasure in each other's company, but nevertheless most satisfying. Friends may be called on to provide a much larger part of the requirements of love and friendship for single people and therefore assume a more important role in their lives.

By drawing on these sources (family and friends), a single person can build a network that will eliminate loneliness and provide the satisfactions of love and friendship.

c. SHOULD YOU MARRY?

Married couples come together for love, and they provide love and companionship for each other. Those who have not married by retirement age have probably remained single by choice and may elect to remain so. But those who were married previously often would prefer to marry again if they found a suitable spouse. There are many advantages. Marrying again can provide the love and companionship as well as financial benefits through the pooling of incomes.

The opportunity is there if you wish to pursue it. There are many potential partners with the same desire; there is someone who would be happy to have you — the trick is to find each other. You have been through this mill before and know the ropes. You succeeded once, you may do so again. Marriage is not only for the young; you have as much to offer to a spouse of your own age now as you had to offer another when you were younger. Once again it will be up to you to get out to see and be seen by potential partners.

d. LIVING ALONE

Living alone has disadvantages. Not only is there no built-in friend to ward off loneliness, but there is the loss of the pleasure of being with someone you enjoy.

There is little incentive to prepare an interesting meal, so you may tend to snack on easily prepared items, not maintain a proper diet and, as a consequence, your health may deteriorate. Those who do not maintain outside contacts may become very introverted and their mental powers may suffer. Alone, life can become a dull, uninteresting existence.

There are many advantages to living with a compatible person. A friend may be the key to your maintaining an interest in things other than yourself, to help in the daily tasks, and to assist in times of illness. Some people fear moving in with a friend because it may encroach on independence and there may be some loss of privacy. It may mean giving up valued possessions that have a cherished link with the past. Compromise on location or other features may be involved. These, however, may be relatively unimportant factors when compared with the advantages.

If you wish to live alone, there is a wide range of arrangements from which to choose, some of which may offer many of the advantages of living with a companion. Friends often take nearby apartments in the same building. Each maintains a private home, but the friends are nearby. They may see each other frequently, visiting is safe and easy, and they assist each other when required.

Group homes, residences that are rented or purchased by a group, are growing in number. Members may have individual rooms but share the common areas, work, and expenses. The final alternative is the retirement home in which meals are provided and housekeeping is done by the staff. Nursing care, entertainment, and hobbies and crafts are included. Residents may come and go as they please, but often group outings with transportation are provided. This is a possible solution for those who cannot continue to live alone and it does have much to offer when needed.

e. LIVING A SATISFACTORY LIFE

The third requirement for happiness is to feel that your life is being well lived, which comes down to a fruitful and satisfying use of time. Each of us has a mental list of things that we must do and standards that we must meet to feel satisfied and retain our personal respect.

These will vary from person to person, but it is important that you recognize yours and that provisions are made to satisfy them. Some may be obligations that may not yield pleasure or fun, but their performance may be essential to peace of mind. From then on you may need an assortment, some for mental and physical health, and others for enjoyment only. Only you can decide what will be needed to provide this satisfaction and peace of mind.

7
MONEY MATTERS

One of the basic requirements for happiness is having enough secure income for a satisfactory life. A life disturbed by financial worries is unlikely to be happy.

There will be many changes to your income at retirement. The money from your regular paycheque will be replaced by money from other sources. Many of your expenditures could be eliminated or reduced, and there are many possibilities of increasing your income. The only people who have no such opportunities are those whose entire incomes will be from fixed pensions, who have no money or significant saleable assets, and who cannot or do not wish to earn additional income.

The next six chapters will show what remains from pre-retirement sources, what new items there may be to add to it, and how your cost of living may change.

This chapter helps you determine how much you currently have to spend after taxation and how you now spend your income. Chapter 8 shows how to estimate your retirement income and includes details of the Old Age Security and Canada Pension Plan. Chapter 9 discusses how to get the most for your money and points out the benefits you will receive, such as government payment of health insurance premiums and extra income tax deductions. Chapter 10 goes into ways that may make all your assets — home, cottage, car, insurance, etc. — work to produce income for you. Chapters 11 and 12 cover handling inflation and retirement savings plans. Each of these chapters contains essential information to help you get all the income you are entitled to and to spend it to the best advantage.

Because your sources of income may be entirely new, the amount perhaps greatly reduced, and the ways in which you spend it very different, it is essential that you make the effort to learn the facts in order to simplify your decision-making.

For example, you may have to choose between two hobbies or activities because of the cost. Often it is possible to eliminate expense without sacrificing much pleasure and, by so doing, to bring your income and expenditures into line. By simply thinking objectively about your expenditures, you may find better ways to save money.

You may be busy and short of time now but once you retire, you will have time to burn and will be seeking useful and profitable ways to employ it. Planning your finances is one of the better ways.

If you dislike this type of work or if you don't think you are able to do it, get the assistance of an accountant. However, first, you must gather certain information about your income and expenses. Your records need not itemize every small detail, but should clearly list all sources of income on a family basis. All expenditures may be grouped in broad classifications that clearly reveal any problems.

a. CALCULATE YOUR TOTAL JOINT INCOME

Be careful not to oversimplify your joint income calculation. Most employed people have some payments made for them by the employer, such as medical insurance, pension plans, company car, etc. If you spend any of your capital or capital gains on living expenses, you should consider this as income.

Begin by listing any income that you or your spouse earn. All you need is paper, a pencil, and, unless you are a good accountant, an eraser. Have some plain paper for doing your rough work and some sheets or a book ruled with horizontal lines and with two vertical columns for dollars and cents on the right of the page. These are available at most stationery stores and will help you organize your work and avoid mistakes.

It is best to calculate a full year's income and expenditures in order to catch all seasonal factors. If you use the last full year, you will also have income records from your employment (T4) slip and an income tax return to use as a check.

First, list all items of income. (See the checklist in section **b.** following.) Once you are retired, many more things come in and go out in monthly units, so it is best to start calculating everything in terms of months. Convert weekly figures to monthly figures by multiplying by $4\frac{1}{3}$ (the average number of weeks in a month).

Some things are paid or billed monthly and no further calculations are necessary. However, many are seasonable or erratic. In such cases, find the total for the year and divide by 12. It will be best to have two columns, annual and monthly, for simplicity and as a check. (See Sample #1.)

Now make up the income side of the picture.

b. YOUR INCOME CHECKLIST

Earned income
Employment earnings (gross) before deductions
Part-time earnings

Income from business
Spouse's earnings
Employer's payments on your behalf

Investment income
Bank interest
Bond interest
Stock dividends
Interest on money lent to others
Capital gains

Other sources of income
Rental income
Room rental or boarders
Car-pool income
Hobby items sold
Service pension
Investments or capital items sold and spent
  rather than saved or reinvested
Gambling gains (losses would go under expenses)
Unemployment insurance received
Family contributions
Other

You may not have income under all of these headings, but list every source you have had in the past year. Otherwise it will seem that you received less money than you actually did and so give a false impression of your annual living costs.

When you have completed the income side, compare it to your last income tax return. This will provide a check against any omission. There may be some items you did not include in your tax return, such as your spouse's income — so make adjustments if necessary. Here are some guides for calculating the entries.

The first item is wages. Calculate and use the gross amount for the year before deductions, and divide by

12 for the monthly figures. Net figures after deductions can be confusing. After retirement, most of your income will be gross — that is, you will receive the full amount without deductions being made at the source. You will then pay any taxes or premiums due directly and these will be different.

Start on this basis now and you can follow it through into your retirement records. The first entry is the gross item from your T4 slips (if employed) divided by 12. If you are self-employed, use your gross drawings before deductions in place of wages.

The next will be income from a second job, if you have one, or from any part-time work you do. Again, take an annual total and calculate the monthly average. As this must be kept on a household basis, record any earnings made by your spouse. This won't be repeated with every item as you go along but, wherever both partners have items of income or expense, list them. It is best to enter them separately and identify each properly so that future checking will be more accurately and easily done.

Now, list investment income. Separate interest on loans, deposits, bonds, and mortgages from common or preferred stock dividends because you classify them differently and pay a lower rate of income tax on dividends from most Canadian corporations. For natural resource industries, there are additional depletion allowances resulting in a lower rate of tax.

Now, consider earnings on property you rent to others. These include income from any property you rent year-round to short-term rentals of your home or cottage. In the latter case, you may list the income here and any corresponding expenses when we come to them.

If you own investment property with several tenants and have a whole list of expenses, it is best to make up a separate statement for the unit and show only net earnings on the income side.

You may have other miscellaneous items. You may have operated a car pool, for example, or sold some craft items at a local show. Everything should be recorded, including gambling winnings or realized capital gains. Losses from gambling or investments (if made up out of current income) are best handled by including them in the expenditures to show where the money went.

The last item catches any remaining income, such as child tax credit, service or other pensions, and income from a trust. If there is any income you have not included under one of the above headings, show it now.

Add it up. Does it look right? If not, first check your addition, then the accuracy of your entries and, finally, if the mistake has not shown up, review each item carefully against your income tax return. When satisfied with the result, you have finished the income side.

To better illustrate the handling of income and expenditures and how they can be manipulated to pay for an enjoyable life in retirement, the incomes, expenditures, and handling of the assets of a mythical couple, John and Mary Jones, make up the following sample.

c. HOW DO YOU SPEND YOUR INCOME?

Now you need to list where your income went. Here is a checklist of the main categories to help you get started.

EXPENSES (WHILE EMPLOYED)

Payroll deductions
Income taxes
Canada Pension Plan

SAMPLE #1
GROSS INCOME WHILE EMPLOYED

ITEM	ANNUAL	MONTHLY
Employment earnings: John	$30 000	$2 500
Employment earnings: Mary	15 000	1 250
Canada Savings Bonds interest: John	1 312	109
Canada Savings Bonds interest: Mary	875	73
Bank interest (joint)	480	40
Earnings from car pool	416	35
TOTAL	$48 083	$4 007

Unemployment insurance
Private pension plan
Union dues
Group insurance
Provincial health and hospital insurance premiums
Private health and hospital insurance premiums
United Appeal
Life (group) insurance

Housing
Rent
Real estate taxes
Heat
Power, water, telephone
TV rental or cable
Mortgage interest
Insurance
Repairs and replacements

Maintenance
Furnishings
Instalment payments
Appliances

Personal
Food
Laundry and cleaning
Life insurance
Clothing
Vacation
Personal care and spending
Recreation
Reading material
Medical (paid directly, not deducted from earnings)
Dental (paid directly, not deducted from earnings)
Public transportation
Gifts and donations

Automobile costs and depreciation

Savings
Payments off mortgage principal
Investments
Savings
Private pension
Life insurance premiums (if there is an increase
   in cash surrender value)

1. Payroll deductions

Start with the payroll deductions. If you are employed,
your T4 slip will show your gross pay and how much
was deducted at the source for unemployment insurance, medical plans, company pension plan, income
tax, and other items. Your income tax returns will show
any additional tax paid or rebates coming to you. If you

had a number of employers during the year, or if you are self-employed, your income tax return is the best place to find these figures as they are likely to be accurate. Record them for both you and your spouse as the first group of expenses.

2. How to calculate the cost of home ownership

The second, and often the largest single item, is the cost of your dwelling. This may be simple to handle if you rent a house or apartment, but it may be much more complex if you own your home. If you rent, enter the monthly rent, then any other expenses that are not included such as power, water, telephone, TV rental, cable, and heat.

If you own your home, rent will not be an entry, but the utilities and the following other expenses will be. The first are the real estate taxes which you can readily ascertain from your tax bill.

The next is the cost of a mortgage. Mortgage payments are generally composed of two or more parts. There are several types of mortgages. The two most common are the conventional and the amortized. You must first find out what type of mortgage you have and what the payments include. These are probably a combination of capital repayment and interest, perhaps taxes and insurance. You must be able to separate these because the capital repayment is a saving, the interest is an expense.

The conventional mortgage often consists of a quarterly interest payment calculated on the principal of the loan outstanding at the beginning of the period. To this is added a regular payment off the principal. Each successive quarterly payment is less because the last payment reduced the principal on which the next quarter's interest is calculated. If the owner of your mortgage or mortgages has not already provided you with a table showing the quarterly payments broken down into principal and interest components, ask for this now.

If the mortgage is amortized, the payments are divided between principal and interest in a different way. A complicated calculation is made once the original amount of the mortgage, the rate of interest, and the final date of repayment has been set. This calculation determines what equal monthly payment of combined interest and principal will be needed for the life of the mortgage so that all the interest and the principal will have been paid off when the last payment is made many years hence.

In an amortized mortgage, the early payments are almost entirely interest, but there are small payments off the principal. The portion coming off the principal increases each time until the final ones are composed of very little interest and a very large portion of principal. Therefore, your expense item will decrease and your saving item increase each year. Again, the mortgage owner should provide you with a breakdown.

If you have a mobile home, you may have the same type of loan used to finance an automobile. However, it doesn't matter what kind it is; the division between interest and principal repayments should be known.

Under mortgage or loan interest, be sure to put the interest payments to be made in the year for which the account is being made up. Farther down, under savings, enter that section of the mortgage or loan payments that is a repayment of the principal.

Next, consider the insurance on your house and perhaps personal property. While this is often referred to as "fire insurance," it frequently protects you against many other risks, such as theft and water damage. Often "personal property" — your clothes, jewellery, furniture, etc. — are included. Read your policy and find out. If you can't understand the wording, ask your agent to explain it. Rather than attempt to separate items into different expenses, record them as one lump sum. If you have a rented home or apartment and do not insure the property but have insurance on your furniture and personal property, include that too.

The expenses for which you are regularly billed are easily ascertained; the estimates are the difficult ones. Soon after a house has been built, repairs are required and these increase over the years. They can range from the simple replacement of washers in leaky faucets to the much more expensive appliance, electrical, or plumbing repairs. Then there is maintenance of the grounds, upkeep, painting, and cleaning. On top of these come the things that may be quite expensive but which will come as surely as the familiar "death and taxes."

Standard roofs have about a 20-year life. Plumbing in older houses, particularly if it is galvanized piping, will have to be replaced. Furnaces and mechanical items will wear out. To estimate these costs, use last year's figures as a guide. If you plan to continue living in your present house, look back over the past few years and see what you have been spending. Then decide if this looks like a reasonable basis on which to project your spending for the next year.

With the estimates and your past experience, you will be able to come up with a reasonably accurate guess. It may be high one year and lower the next, but you will be prepared for the expenses as they come for they will average out over the years. If possible, have all major repairs and replacements completed and paid for before retirement.

The next item to consider is heat. If you have an accurate record of past bills, you can use those figures. If you do not, the oil or gas company can tell you your last year's total and whether an increase is forthcoming.

If you are in a condominium or a co-op apartment, rent a mobile home lot, or have some arrangement different from those discussed above, get a figure that covers all the related costs, including such things as membership in the organization.

3. Personal expenses

Under personal expenses, start by calculating food cost. If you pay cash for your groceries, you may not have any records to look back on, but a little thought on your part can tie it down fairly accurately.

Most families follow a certain shopping routine — perhaps a major trip once a week. Keep all sales slips for each week for one year. Soon you will not only have an accurate figure, but you may also learn some interesting things about controlling your food costs. Remember to add any meals usually purchased away from home to this total.

Estimating clothing expense is more difficult because it doesn't usually follow a regular monthly pattern. If you can, estimate over a period of years the average annual expenditure required to keep up your wardrobes.

Laundry and cleaning bills can be estimated next. Don't forget the seasonal bulges that occur when putting away winter and summer clothes.

4. Automobile costs and depreciation

Automobile costs require thought and accuracy. Perhaps you have a charge account that covers regular running expenses and repairs, tires, batteries, etc. If not, make a very honest estimate here. Adjust for rising prices if necessary.

Now, list instalment payments if your car is financed. As with a mortgage, these payments will be a combination of principal repayments and interest. Ask for a breakdown from the finance company. Include the principal repayments as savings; the interest paid goes under expenses.

The annual decrease in your car's value due to aging will be taken care of by depreciation. Depreciation is the estimated decrease in the value of the car during a certain period, say one year, because you have used up some of the car's available mileage and the model is now one year older. It is not a cash cost this year — you paid it out when you bought the car. It simply means that, when sold or traded, the car will bring less than its original price. The difference is the depreciation and, when calculating an annual cost, this figure should be estimated and included.

Accurate records over the years indicate that a car, on average, depreciates at the rate of about 30% per year. That means 30% of its value at the beginning of the year is used up in the year, and this must be subtracted from the value to obtain a figure with which to start the following year. The next depreciation is taken from this reduced figure and, thus, the depreciation declines each year. However, repairs increase often almost as quickly as depreciation declines.

Assume that you are driving a car that cost $8 000. The yearly cost of depreciation is calculated by taking

30% of the value at the beginning of that year. Thus, for the first year it is $2 400. In the second year the calculation is made by deducting the $2 400 from the $8 000, that is, $5 600, and then taking 30% of that, which is $1 680. For the third year and successive years, continue on in the same manner.

At the end of the fifth year, the remaining (depreciated) value of the car is $1 344, and the total depreciation for the five-year-period is $6 656, or an annual average of $1 331. (This is the figure you would use in your estimated costs.)

Now add in the licence, operating, and insurance costs and you have a total for the year.

If you have capital tied up in your car, that money might earn 10% interest or more in investments, so you are foregoing at least 10% income for every $1 000 invested in your car. Keep that in mind for future reference, but do not enter it in this calculation.

Sample #2 shows an example of calculating auto expenses. Replace these figures with your own.

d. THE FINAL LIST

Sample #3 shows how one couple might use their means; it is not presented as a goal to which you, personally, should strive. The money accumulated during the year would actually be greater than the savings shown in the sample because the automobile expense of $3 456 includes $1 331 for depreciation. This is not money paid out this year but represents the decrease in value of the car during the year. This money should be saved to be available to purchase a new car when the present one is traded in.

SAMPLE #2
ESTIMATED AUTOMOBILE EXPENSES

Consider a car that cost $8 000 five years ago

Estimated annual driving:
16 000 km of combined city and country driving

Depreciation calculated as above	$1 331
Licence	50
Insurance	750
Gasoline, oil, lubrication, etc.	1 050
Repairs, replacement	275
Annual Total	**$3 456**

Note: If the $8 000 had been invested it might earn $480 per year. If this is considered part of the expense of ownership, it then totals $3 936.

SAMPLE #3
HOW THE MONEY WAS SPENT

ITEM	ANNUAL	MONTHLY
Deductions and taxes		
Income tax deducted from paycheque: John	$4 588	$382
Income tax deducted from paycheque: Mary	1 509	126
Taxes paid direct	253	21
Other payroll deductions	1 080	90
Utilities		
Power, water, TV rental	650	54
Telephone (home and cottage)	300	25
Home		
Real estate taxes	1 950	164
Heat	950	79
Repairs and maintenance	775	64
Insurance	525	44
Furnishings	700	58
Appliances	325	27
Cottage		
Taxes	1 100	93
Insurance	500	542
Power	225	18
Repairs and maintenance	850	71
Personal		
Food and meals	6 125	510
Laundry and cleaning	350	29
Clothing	2 080	173
Vacation	1 100	92
Recreation	1 500	125
Reading	200	17
Personal care	600	500
Medical and dental (not insured)	425	35
Life insurance premium	162	13
Automobile: John	3 456	288
Automobile: Mary	3 456	288
Gifts and donations	400	33
Contributions to RRSP		
John	5 400	450
Mary	2 700	225
Savings	3 849	321
TOTAL	$48 083	$4 007

85

8
ESTIMATING RETIREMENT INCOME

Now that you have completed a list of last year's earnings and expenditures, you are ready to prepare an estimate of your post-retirement income. You will then have an accurate picture of your financial position and will know what changes, if any, will be necessary. Use the same form as previously, but now you will have to replace your salary with new sources of income.

a. IMPORTANT BIRTHDAYS

There are two birthdays that bring prizes that make winning one of those $100-a-month-for-life awards look small! Both are landmarks and will be significant in your decision of when to retire.

1. Your 60th birthday

(a) On the day you turn 60, you may elect to begin drawing on the Canada or Quebec Pension Plans as long as you are otherwise eligible (see sections **h.** and **i.** following).

(b) If you are the spouse, widow, or widower of an Old Age Pensioner and are between 60 and 65 with income below the maximum, you may be eligible for a Spouse's Allowance (see section **c.** following).

(c) Many age-related discounts begin. In total, they can add up to a tidy sum.

2. Your 65th birthday

(a) You may be eligible for the Old Age Security pension of $378.19 per month (as of October 1, 1992, increasing quarterly). If your spouse is between 60 and 65, he or she may be eligible for the Spouse's Allowance (see the sections on Old Age Security and Spouse's Allowance following).

(b) The "Clawback" or "Social Benefits Repayment" was, in 1991, a 15% tax on taxable income above $51 765 until the tax yielded a sum equal to the Old Age Security received. The base amount is subject to indexing in future years.

(c) The Guaranteed Income Supplement — Single or married persons who are entitled to the full Old Age Security and whose income from other sources does not exceed specified amounts may be entitled to the Guaranteed Income Supplement. If you receive partial Old Age Security you may qualify for a partial supplement. Contact your local Income Security Programs office for information.

The larger your income, the smaller the supplement you will receive.

	Income	Monthly Supplement
Single	Nil	$449.44
	$10 799.99	.44
Married	Nil	$280.50 each
	$14 063.99	.75

(d) Your spouse may qualify at age 60 for a Spouse's Allowance, that is, all or part of the Old Age Security Pension, depending on your combined incomes. While there is no income test for the Old Age Security at age 65, there is for the Guaranteed Income Supplement at that age, and the Spouse's Allowance is payable to *either a husband or wife* provided the other partner receives the Old Age Security Pension and meets all other requirements. The Spouse's Allowance is no longer discontinued if the spouse receiving the pension dies.

(e) A widow or widower may be eligible for a Widowed Spouse's Allowance, provided he or she is between 60 and 65 and has an income below $14 807.99. The maximum payment for those with no income is $740.71 per month.

(f) The premium for your provincial health and hospital plan (which varies in each province) will be eliminated. Most drug costs may be paid by your province (prescription only).

(g) The provinces and municipalities have support programs of many kinds, offering financial support and assistance in other ways. Enquire at your local level.

Note: You must have a social insurance number to receive any government pensions or other forms of assistance. If you do not have one, apply at once. Forms are available at banks, post offices, and Canada Employment Centres.

b. CHECKLIST FOR INCOME SOURCES

1. Pensions

(a) Old Age Security Pension

(b) Guaranteed Income Supplement

(c) Spouse's and Widowed Spouse's Allowance

(d) Provincial assistance

(e) Canada or Quebec Pension

(f) Private or industrial pension

(g) Service pension

2. **Investment income**

(a) Bank interest

(b) Bonds and other interest

(c) Dividends from Canadian stocks

(d) Net income from investment property

(e) Room rentals or boarders

(f) Income from foreign sources

(g) Capital gains

(h) Other

3. **Earned income**

(a) Hobby income

(b) Employment earnings

c. THE OLD AGE SECURITY PENSION

The Old Age Security Pension is paid as a matter of right to all eligible persons. To be eligible, you must be at least 65, have Canadian legal residence status, and meet residence requirements. You do not need to be retired, and there is no income test as there is with the Spouse's Allowance and the Guaranteed Income Supplement.

A birth or baptismal certificate is requested, but if one is not available, there are other acceptable forms of proof. If you do not have either certificate, visit a local Income Security Programs office to discuss your case.

A new Old Age Security Act came into force July 1, 1977. The old act remains in force for certain people, the new for others. The old act still applies to —

(a) those now drawing pensions (who will be unaffected), and

(b) legal Canadian residents now over 25 years of age who have resided in Canada at any time since attaining the age of 18, or who possess a valid immigration visa dated prior to July 1, 1977.

1. Residence requirements (under the old act)

Residence requirements are met if you —

(a) have resided in Canada after reaching the age of 18 for periods that total at least 40 years,

(b) have resided or been in Canada for 10 consecutive years immediately before approval of the application,

(c) have been present in Canada after reaching the age of 18 and prior to the 10 years mentioned above, for periods that equal at least three times the length of absence during the 10-year period and have resided in Canada for at least 1 year immediately preceding the approval of your application,

(d) are a legal Canadian resident.

2. The new Old Age Security Act

The new act applies to —

(a) new immigrants whose visas are dated after July 1, 1977,

(b) Canadian residents under the age of 25 on July 1, 1977, and

(c) those who cannot qualify under the old act but may under the new one, and choose to do so.

The following are changes made under the new act.

(a) The applicant must be a legal resident of Canada.

(b) Application may now be made from outside Canada provided the applicant has resided in Canada for 20 years. (This makes the Old Age Security Pension available to some former residents now living abroad who could not qualify unless they came back to Canada and lived here for one year immediately prior to making application.)

(c) The Old Age Security Pension is earned year by year. Previously, if you qualified, you received the full pension. Now you "earn" it as follows: $\frac{1}{40}$ of the pension for each year of legal residence in Canada after the age of 18. Thus, a qualified applicant with 20 years' residence would qualify for $\frac{20}{40}$ or $\frac{1}{2}$ of the maximum pension. The maximum pension and provision for indexing are the same as under the old act.

(d) The applicant must have lived in Canada for a minimum of 10 years after the age of 18.

Application forms are available at post offices and Income Security Programs offices. They should be submitted six months before you turn 65, so that your pension will start in the month following your birthday.

3. What is the Spouse's Allowance?

This program is designed to provide additional income if a couple is living on a single Old Age Pension. It does not, therefore, apply in the case of married couples where both spouses are between the ages of 60 and 65.

91

The act provides for payment of a monthly benefit to spouses of Old Age Security pensioners provided —

(a) one spouse gets the Old Age Security Pension,

(b) the applying spouse is between 60 and 65,

(c) the combined income of the couple does not exceed $20 159.99 (as of October, 1992) exclusive of Old Age Security payments, Guaranteed Income Supplement, and Spouse's Allowance.

(d) Spouse's Allowance may be payable to the spouse of the deceased pensioner if the survivor's income is less than $14 807.99 per annum.

If the cost of living rises, as measured by the consumer price index, the combined income under which a spouse may qualify for the Spouse's Allowance increases. Payments are reduced as the couple's combined income increases until the maximum income figure is reached, at which point no allowance is payable. In addition, you should apply under the following circumstances:

(a) Your combined income exceeds the maximum by a small amount, for there may be exclusions you are unaware of and as the maximum increases quarterly you may soon become eligible

(b) Within six months of your 60th birthday, if residence and financial requirements are met, and your spouse is or will be receiving the Old Age Security Pension within that time

4. Payment of the Old Age Security Pension

Payment can begin in the month after your 65th birthday. If you are late applying, it can be paid for five years retroactively. The monthly payment is now subject to change and is adjusted quarterly with the cost of living.

Once approved, pension payments may be made to you outside Canada indefinitely if you have resided in Canada for at least 20 years after your 18th birthday. If you do not meet these qualifications, the pension will be paid outside Canada for six months only.

d. THE GUARANTEED INCOME SUPPLEMENT (GIS)

As of October, 1992, you may be eligible for all or part of the Guaranteed Income Supplement if —

(a) You are single, separated, widowed, or divorced and your yearly income apart from the Old Age Pension is less than $10 799.99.

(b) You are married, and you and your spouse are both receiving the pension, and your combined yearly income apart from the Old Age Pension is less than $14 063.99.

(c) You are married, and your spouse is not a pensioner and is not eligible for a Spouse's Allowance, and your combined yearly income apart from the Old Age Pension is less than $26 159.99.

(d) You are married and either you or your spouse is a pensioner, and your husband or wife is between 60 and 65 years of age, you may be eligible for a supplement and your husband or wife for a Spouse's Allowance if your combined yearly income is less than $20 159.99 and your spouse can meet the residence requirements.

(e) You are widowed and entitled to a Spouse's Allowance, you may be eligible for a supplement if your annual income is less than $14 807.99.

When you apply for Old Age Security Pension, an application for the Guaranteed Income Supplement will be sent to you. The maximum monthly supplement for October, 1992, was $449.44 for a single person and $292.75 each for couples. The payments increase quarterly with the Old Age Security payment increases.

For purposes of calcualting your income, government payments that are not considered income for tax purposes are not included as income.

Note: The Old Age Security Pension must be included in taxable income but the Spouse's Allowance and Guaranteed Income Supplement are not.

e. INTERNATIONAL AGREEMENTS FOR FOREIGN PENSIONS

Many Canadians have worked in other countries and hold credits in their pension plans. Canada has Reciprocal International Social Security Agreements with a number of countries.

Canada has agreements in force or pending ratification with these countries:

- Australia

- Austria

- Barbados

- Belgium

- Denmark

- Dominica

- Finland

- France

- Greece

- Iceland

- Italy

- Jamaica

- Luxembourg

- The Netherlands

- Norway

- Portugal

- Saint Lucia

- Spain

- Sweden

- Germany

- U.S.A.

In some cases, foreign pensions get special tax treatment in Canada. For example, Canada taxes only half of a U.S. social security payment.

Your local Health and Welfare office can provide more information.

f. PROVINCIAL ASSISTANCE

If you do not qualify for benefits under the Canada Pension Plan and are in need, or if the benefits you receive under the Canada Pension Plan, Old Age Security Pension, and Guaranteed Income Supplement Program are insufficient to meet your needs, you should write to or call your provincial welfare department in the capital city of your province for information about the additional assistance that may be available to you.

Regulations for eligibility and amounts payable change rapidly, so you should inquire about current regulations for the province you live in or for any you anticipate moving to. There are many other benefits available at either the provincial or municipal level.

g. PROVINCIAL PLANS

The Saskatchewan Pension Plan (SPP) is a voluntary savings fund. It was created in 1986 for those with no employer's pension, although it's open to any provincial resident aged 18 to 65. The Saskatchewan government matches contributions made by low income members.

In its 1990 speech from the Throne, the British Columbia government promised a provincial pension plan. The speech expressed particular concern for homemakers who lack employer plans.

British Columbia, Alberta, Saskatchewan, Manitoba, Ontario, Nova Scotia, the Yukon and the Northwest Territories pay special benefits to low-income pensioners who qualify for the federal GIS payment. Like GIS, these payments are tax-free.

h. THE CANADA PENSION PLAN

The Canada Pension Plan is separate from, and in addition to, the Old Age Security Pension. They have nothing to do with each other and, if you are eligible, you and your spouse can have both.

The Canada Pension Plan applies in all parts of Canada with the exception of Quebec, where the Quebec

Pension Plan takes its place. Some benefits differ between the two plans (see Table #1).

In addition to the pension, there are provisions for death benefits and pensions for a surviving spouse and dependent children. There are also possible disability benefits for a contributor who is disabled but not yet drawing a pension.

Eligibility rules for Canada Pension Plan are as follows:

(a) You must have worked in "pensionable employment" as defined by the Canada Pension Plan and have paid premiums into the fund at some time, but not necessarily all the time, since January 1, 1966.

(b) You must have a social insurance number.

1. Making the application

You may now apply for the Canada Pension Plan any time between your 60th and 70th birthdays. To apply between ages 60 and 64, you must have "substantially ceased working."

Between ages 65 and 70 the applicant does not have to cease employment, but once the pension payments begin, no further payments can be made to the plan. Annual adjustments to reflect changes in the Consumer Price Index will be made annually.

The monthly pension cheque to which you are entitled will be based on a number of items, the first being your pensionable earnings. This will be the total amount of pensionable earnings on which you have paid premiums since the inception of the plan in 1966. (Note it is this amount, not the premiums, that is used in the calculation.)

The original plan required that annual earnings exceeded $600 if the person was employed and $800 if self-employed. These minimums have been increased from time to time. Premiums were paid originally according to a schedule of earnings up to $5 000. Any excess earnings over the maximum allowable in any year were not included. This figure has been increased regularly and it reached $32 200 in 1992. By law this figure will increase by 12½% per annum until it reaches the industrial composite wage index.

Every time this figure is increased, it, in effect, increases all future pensions not yet started, for the pensionable earnings used to calculate these pensions will not be the original ones, but will be new ones, greatly increased. These calculations are made for you and every increase will automatically increase your starting pension. Your pension will be 25% of your adjusted average pensionable earnings that you reported from January 1, 1966 until the month before your pension starts. There are provisions to eliminate or replace certain months of no or low earnings that might reduce the pension.

If your earnings have not been up to the maximum pensionable amount, your pension will be the same percentage of the maximum pension as your earnings were of the maximum pensionable earnings.

Application should be made six months before the desired starting date. Payments cannot begin until the month after application and they cannot be backdated, unless you are over 70, in which case there are certain provisions to allow you to do so.

2. The monthly cheque

During 1992, the maximum monthly cheque payable to those eligible and to those who started drawing it on their 65th birthday is $636.11. Those whose contributions were below the maximum receive a proportionately smaller amount.

If you choose a starting date before your 65th birthday, the pension will be calculated as if it were your 65th birthday but for every month of your age less than 65, the cheque will be reduced by ½ of 1% (or 6% per year). If you are 60 when you apply for the pension, the figure would be reduced by 30%.

If you start drawing the pension between 65 and 70, the pension will be increased by ½ of 1% for every month of your age more than 65, but it cannot be increased by more than 30%.

If you are employed past age 65, your employer may deduct premiums, but they may be refundable. Ask for details at your local Income Security office.

3. Check your record of contribution

Your premiums and employment records are the base on which your pension will be calculated. If these records are incorrect, you may not receive what you are entitled to, and errors or omissions left unattended may be difficult to correct. To guard against this, the pension department now sends all Canadians copies of their records every three years for review. If you have not received one, you can inquire at your local Income Security office. When you do receive your form, ask your employer for verification and if there are any errors, ask to have them corrected at once.

Take your form to your local Income and Security office, Department of Health and Welfare or, if you live in Quebec, to the Regie des Rentes du Quebec. They will be able to tell you what pensions you might expect at various ages, alert you to any options and advise what protection your spouse and family are entitled to, and assure you that your records are in order. These offices should be contacted for any other matters relating to your pension.

4. What is the best age to apply?

When you apply will depend on when you wish to retire and when you want the income. The later you start, the larger the monthly cheque will be. This decision can only be made as part of your total calculations of retirement income and expenditures.

Keep in mind that if you have not contributed to the plan for long enough to qualify your spouse and children for survivors' pensions if you die, you may want to continue working until you have done so. Your local Income Security office will be able to advise you on your position.

5. What benefits are payable if you die?

(a) Death benefit

If you have contributed for the lesser of 10 calendar years or one-third of the years possible since January 1, 1966 or since age 18 if that came later, a death benefit is payable to your estate when you die. This benefit amounts to six months of the retirement pension if one is being paid or, if not, of a pension calculated as if you became 65 at the date of death. (This cannot exceed 10% of the maximum pensionable earnings figure for the year of death, and for 1992 it was $3 220). The pensioner need not have reached 65 at the time of death.

(b) Spouse's pension

A pension may be payable to your husband or wife when you die (see details, chapter 13).

(c) Dependants' pensions

Dependants' pensions may be payable to dependent children.

6. Disability pension

Who can be considered disabled? For the purpose of the Canada Pension Plan, a contributor is not deemed to be disabled unless he or she has a physical or mental impairment that is both severe and prolonged — severe in the sense that the person is incapable of regularly pursuing any substantially gainful employment and prolonged in the sense that the disability, in all likelihood, will be long, continuous, and of indefinite duration, or is likely to result in death. This is determined by a test of a contributor's disability and inability to work. The disability need not be caused by injury, but can also result from illness which is not necessarily caused by employment.

A contributor cannot receive a disability pension and a retirement pension at the same time. If the contributor is between 60 and 65, either pension could be payable. The disability pension is made up of a flat-rate portion and an earnings-related portion. The maximum disability pension in 1992 was $783.99.

7. Separation or divorce

Specific provisions apply to the division of pension benefits if you are separated or divorced from a legal or common-law marriage. The terms also vary depending on whether or not the separation or divorce took place after January 1, 1987. Some divisions are mandatory and others are optional, but no division of credits will be made if —

(a) the Minister of National Health and Welfare is satisfied that it would be to the detriment of both spouses, or

(b) one or both of the spouses contributed to the Quebec Pension Plan during the period of cohabitation unless a division is permitted under both the Quebec and Canada Pension Plans.

If you are affected by a separation or divorce, contact the Income Security office for advice.

8. Working parents

A parent may drop out of paid pensionable employment to care for children under the age of seven without losing Canada Pension Plan benefits that would have accumulated had he or she remained in the work force.

i. THE QUEBEC PENSION PLAN

The Quebec Pension Plan takes the place of the Canada Pension Plan in Quebec. It has the same basic eligibility requirements and provisions as the Canada Pension Plan. However, there are some differences. The retirement pensions and death benefits are the same, but the others vary. (See Table #1.)

j. MOVING FROM ONE PLAN TO THE OTHER

If you have contributed to the Quebec Pension Plan only, your pension application must be made to Quebec, and your pension will be issued by Quebec, regardless of where you reside when you apply.

On the other hand, if you have contributed to both plans at any time, your application must be made to the plan in effect in the province or territory in which you are residing at the date of your application. This means

TABLE #1
MAXIMUM MONTHLY BENEFITS UNDER THE
CANADA AND QUEBEC PENSION PLANS

Type of benefit	Beneficiary's age	CPP	QPP
Retirement	60	$445.28	$445.28
	61	483.44	483.44
	62	521.66	521.66
	63	559.78	559.78
	64	597.94	597.94
	65	636.11	636.11
	66	674.28	674.28
	67	712.44	712.44
	68	750.61	750.61
	69	788.78	788.78
	70+	826.44	826.44
Disability	Under 65	783.89	783.89
	Over 65	Replaced by retirement pension	Replaced by retirement pension
Surviving widow/er of pensioner	65 or over	381.67	381.67
	65 and under	352.71	352.71
	55-65	631.06	631.06
	Under 55	545.35	545.35

No benefit payable under 35 without a child.

Death benefit (single payment) $3 220 $3 220

There are also benefits for a disabled contributor's child and for orphans. For further information contact Health and Welfare Canada or Régie des rentes du Québec.

that if you have contributed to only one plan and you wish to draw the pension from the other, you could establish residence in the desired jurisdiction and, provided you make one valid contribution to the new plan and apply from that point, you could draw the pension from it.

All contributions to both plans are transferred to the one from which the pension is drawn and, once it has commenced, it will continue to be issued from that source and will be governed by its rules. The process is not reversible.

You should note that there is an annual maximum pensionable earnings figure in both plans, and once you have paid premiums on that amount, no further premiums can be paid to either plan in that year. Thus, if you moved at that point, you might have to wait until the next calendar year to be eligible to establish an attachment to the desired plan.

k. PRIVATE OR INDUSTRIAL PENSION PLANS

You may have either a personal or an industrial pension plan or both. Find out well before retirement exactly what these plans offer.

Some have options and you must make a choice. Do not do this without knowing, studying, and understanding the long-term effects your decision will have.

In the case of an industrial plan that comes with your job, you should ask through appropriate channels just what the pension offers. Don't be satisfied with verbal information; get the facts in writing. Take them away, study them, and discuss them with your spouse, accountant, lawyer, and/or advisor.

If it is a personal pension from an insurance company, you will have a legal contract that was given to you when you purchased it. Study this and ask advice as suggested above. Check with the insurance company to see if there are any improvements to be offered. Consider any alternatives from which you must choose on retirement. Above all, don't make a final decision without studying your whole retirement plan and taking your spouse's situation into account should he or she outlive you. This is discussed in chapter 13.

1. INVESTMENT AND OTHER INCOME

Income from previously owned investments, room rentals, etc., will continue on and are not directly affected by retirement. They can be carried into your retirement income estimate unchanged. Some income, such as that from your car pool, will cease with employment.

If you anticipate new sources of income after retirement, include them, but be careful. Jobs for retired people are scarce, have little security, and usually offer less pay than they would for full-time younger people. Don't count on this unless you have a job lined up.

Hobby income is also speculative. If you are now earning income from it and can reasonably expect it to continue or increase, fine. If not, do work toward its development, but don't count on it to buy the groceries.

m. PRELIMINARY ESTIMATE OF RETIREMENT INCOME

John and Mary are about to retire; both are 65. Like most Canadians, neither will receive a pension from their employers. Both are eligible for Canada and Old Age Security Pensions. Their children are now independent.

As a retiring employee, you will be entitled to holiday pay and, perhaps, other items. Be sure and ask your employer. If these items do not fill the gap, you should prepare for it by saving. In any case, you should know what to expect.

SAMPLE #4
ESTIMATE OF RETIREMENT INCOME 1992

ITEM	ANNUAL
Canada Pension Plan: John	$6 900
Canada Pension Plan: Mary	3 900
Old Age Security: John	4 509
Old Age Security: Mary	4 509
Canada Savings Bonds interest: John	1 500
Canada Savings Bonds interest: Mary	1 000
Bank interest	480
TOTAL	$22 798

9
YOUR COST OF LIVING IN RETIREMENT

With your statement of retirement income in hand, you can now decide what you can afford. You need to know how you are going to live and the cost of your choices. The changes made in your way of living may make a significant difference in your expenses. To know what these are requires careful thought. There are reductions in three areas.

(a) *Age-related costs*: Provincial acceptance of all or part of health care costs at 65, etc.

(b) *Employment related costs*: Union dues, pension payments, etc., cease.

(c) *Lifestyle costs*: Many discounts are offered to seniors; also, you may turn former expenses into income.

The list of expenditures you made while working is out of date because of these changes, but it will provide basic, valuable information for making decisions now.

The first step is to list your expected expenses in retirement, using the figures of your present costs as a guide, but adjusting each for changes that can be predicted. We will examine these to see what to expect.

a. INCOME TAX RESPONSIBILITIES

If 75% or more of your income has been from employment, income tax has been deducted at the source and any balance due has been paid when you filed your

108

annual return. However, now, if over 25% of your income comes from sources at which deductions have not been made, and it probably will after retirement, you are required to make quarterly instalments if you are liable for over $1 000 in tax.

If you do have a part-time job and taxes have been deducted, the full pay should be recorded in your income and all deductions recorded in your expense schedule. Even if some deductions are made at source, unless they are taken from at least three-quarters of your income, you may be responsible for making quarterly instalments on the balance.

You would be wise to discuss these liabilities with a tax advisor. If you do not have such a connection, do not hesitate to contact your local tax office. They are most helpful and you have nothing to fear as they will give all information freely without asking your name. They are courteous and try to assist as much as possible.

Warning: Approaching the tax office on simple matters is all right but be wary of seeking advice on more complex matters. Because of the complexities of the Income Tax Act, it is best to seek expert advice.

b. DO NOT LET THEM LAPSE!

Once you are retired, the benefits your employer deducted from your paycheque cease and you must reinstate them directly if you wish them to continue. If you are not old enough to qualify for free provincial medical/hospital care, you must pay the premiums for them yourself. You may have been receiving extra coverage through extended hospital, dental, or drug plans, which, again, will lapse if you do not pay the premiums. You also may have had optional life insurance coverage that you will want to continue after you retire. You

109

should be sure to ask your employer for all the pertinent information about these matters before you leave work.

c. YOUR HOME

The next cost to consider is your dwelling. If you continue to live in the same home, you can simply use the expense calculations made in your first schedule with any estimate for expected changes. If you move later, you can make the change in a final calculation.

Some municipalities have special property tax deferrals for owners above a certain age. Check to see if yours has this provision.

In making your forecast of retirement plans, you should realize that advancing years may require some difference in your estimate. Will you be able to continue to do some of the heavier chores? If not, include the cost of having someone do them for you.

d. EATING FOR HEALTH AND PLEASURE

Eating can be a most enjoyable experience, yet retired people who are not usually cooking to please a hungry family often lose interest in food. As a result, they may rely on tea and toast or similar easily prepared things. By doing so, they lose the opportunity of having an enjoyable experience, and they may not get the necessary nourishment required to maintain health.

Younger people eat more and, therefore, are more likely to get all the protein, minerals, and vitamins required along with the calories to provide the energy needed. The older person requires fewer calories for energy, but still needs at least as much of the other nutrients as before. As you reduce the quantity of food eaten, you may need a better selection; this is still possible with simple, easily prepared meals.

The starting point is finding out whether your current diet is adequate. There are several ways of doing this: ask your doctor for suggestions and advice, call your local health office and ask if there is a qualified nutritionist or nurse available who can provide the information, or read some of the excellent material available either from the health office or the library. You may find that by reading you can make up new, interesting, enjoyable meals, keep control of costs, and add a new zest to eating.

Now that you have the time, why not make this a project and see how much pleasure it can provide? Try new things and look at cooking as a source of pleasure rather than a chore. Rapidly increasing food costs may be a problem, and using replacements for the very high-cost items may be a good way to control them; shop to take advantage of specials or items in season when they cost less. Remember, the aim is not just to cut cost, but to eat well and enjoyably at the same time. By planning and buying carefully, you may be able to have some of those things that you really enjoy, even if they are high priced.

Dining out is less expensive at lunch, and often the menu is lighter and more suitable for seniors. Why not invite a friend and make it a social outing too? Some retired people find pleasure in forming a small dinner club that meets regularly. It is an event to look forward to and a chance to eat someone else's cooking. Retired men often take a new interest in cooking; they may become experts and take great pleasure in preparing dishes that appeal to them.

The opportunities are there: make eating a pleasure, and at the same time provide the nourishment you need for your health and happiness.

e. CLOTHING

Clothing costs also may be reduced, for work often requires a standard of dress you need not maintain during retirement. You may have the time to make some of your clothes now, which will save you substantial funds and provide you with an interesting hobby at the same time. Once again, the changes made depend on your personal circumstances, so make the best estimate you can. Laundry and cleaning costs may also be reduced.

f. ENTERTAINMENT

You may wish to spend more time with hobbies and enjoy additional entertainment because you have more time available, but this doesn't mean you need to spend more money. First, you no longer need to go to shows at the expensive times, like Friday and Saturday nights. You can go on "off" nights and to matinees. Rather than going out for dinner, you and your friends might enjoy a leisurely lunch. Now that you have more time, you may do more entertaining at home as well. Further, you will save by taking advantage of the lower prices so often given to seniors. Also look into special group rates.

g. VACATIONS AND TRAVEL

There are many basic savings now available to you in the travel area.

(a) Select off-peak season dates which are usually substantially cheaper.

(b) Notice that certain days of departure and return are often much less expensive on airlines and other carriers.

(c) Consider vacation periods that are often not possible for the working person and may be more reasonably priced.

(d) Resorts may give a discount if it is requested. Inquire; you shouldn't pay full price when it is not necessary.

(e) Public carriers often give reduced rates to seniors.

(f) Look for less expensive rather than the glamour spots. For example, in winter, accommodation on the northern gulf coast of Florida often costs as little as one-quarter of a similar place farther south.

(g) Look for less expensive group plans.

h. ELIMINATE INSTALMENT PAYMENTS

Instalment payments are generally used to purchase larger, more expensive items of furniture, clothing, or, perhaps, an automobile. At this stage in your life, it may be that you will have the option of delaying such purchases. While instalment purchases may be desirable, or necessary, they often include an interest charge at a very high rate.

Now the desire to eliminate unnecessary costs and obtain the most for every dollar calls for the end of expensive borrowing. Save for major purchases, but if you do borrow, do so on the best security you have to obtain the lowest rate.

i. MEDICAL AND DENTAL

The basic health plan will be paid for you once you or your spouse is eligible for Old Age Security Pension, but there are usually some unavoidable expenses not covered by any insurance. You may elect to purchase a private plan to provide extra protection. Enter an estimate for these added costs and all known medical expenses plus a fair estimate for others that will probably come. Overall, there should be a reduction of substantial proportions in this category.

j. TRANSPORTATION

Now that travel requirements such as going to work and driving children about are past, many of you can take a new look at transportation requirements. The operating cost of an automobile is very high, and many "two-car" couples find they are able to manage with one car during retirement. Others dispose of cars completely; public transportation is often less expensive and almost all public carriers give discounts to pensioners. For example, the TTC in Toronto sells pensioner tickets at half price; in Vancouver there is a discount with proper identification; in Calgary there are discounts and special arrangements even on taxi fares. Airlines and railways have discounts at certain times. The combined use of public transportation and rental cars for special occasions may be satisfactory. Consider these factors again if you decide to relocate your home.

If you do decide to keep your automobile, costs will follow the same basic calculations made previously but, if you have driven to work, you will now automatically eliminate this driving. However, do not underestimate the rapidly escalating costs of running an automobile. Retired people often make a basic change in automobile usage and, therefore, in the annual cost. This may be possible if you foresee a substantial reduction in mileage. In addition to gasoline and oil, repairs and replacements are closely related to mileage. Depreciation is quite high in the early years but it decreases rapidly over time. Insurance, licence, garage, and other similar expenses, however, will remain constant.

The simple reduction of your mileage may substantially reduce the annual running costs. If, for example, you now expect to cut your mileage in half, you could keep the car twice as long, and your average annual depreciation would be much lower.

If you reduce your mileage to 5 000 miles (8 000 km) per year by eliminating that drive to work, and you are able to keep your car twice as long or until it has gone 50 000 miles (80 000 km) (a 10-year period), your average depreciation would be reduced by half each year.

With just you and your spouse using the car and the need to cut costs, it might be best for you to purchase a smaller car that requires less gasoline. As well, a less expensive car will have a lower depreciation rate and other operating costs.

k. BANK CHARGES

Most banks will grant discounts for some services to people over 60. These often include a discount for depositors renting safety deposit boxes, free chequing privileges, a bonus on interest earned to help keep up with inflation, and no service charge for some utility bill payments. Ask your manager what discounts or free services are available to you.

The cost of services may be lower if made through an Automatic Teller rather than over the counter. Ask your branch for details.

1. EVALUATE EACH EXPENDITURE AGAIN

Now total your expected expenses and compare them with the anticipated income. How does it look? Is your income adequate? If it is and you have listed all the things you wish to do, there is no problem. However, if there is not enough income to cover the expenses or there are still things that you had hoped to be able to afford but you did not include, you should now investigate the possible ways of increasing income and reducing expenditures, eliminating those items that provide little satisfaction. There are plenty of opportunities to make painless adjustments.

It is time you reviewed each expenditure seriously and judged it by your new lifestyle. Does it make a worthwhile contribution to the welfare and happiness of you and your spouse now that you are retired?

When you review your list again, challenge every item and justify each carefully. If you cannot, eliminate it. (See Sample #5, which shows how John and Mary estimated their retirement costs.)

John and Mary had hoped to spend five months each year at their cottage where they played golf, fished, and enjoyed rural life. The remainder of the year would be spent at their home where they both had interests.

When they compared their expected living costs of $33 618 to their income of $22 698, it was obvious that their chosen lifestyle was impossible. They had to find ways to reduce costs and/or increase income to provide a balance that would pay for a lifestyle as close as possible to what they had planned.

The next chapter looks at some possibilities for increasing income.

SAMPLE #5
ESTIMATED COST OF LIVING IN RETIREMENT

ITEM	ANNUAL	MONTHLY
Income taxes to pay direct		
John:	$2 704	$225
Mary:	979	82
Utilities		
Power, water, TV rental	650	54
Telephone	325	27
House expense		
Real estate taxes	2 150	179
Heat	1 000	83
Insurance	600	50
Repairs & maintenance	800	67
Furnishings	500	42
Appliances	325	27
Cottage		
Real estate taxes	1 200	100
Insurance	500	42
Power	250	21
Repairs & maintenance	850	71
Personal		
Food and restaurants	5 950	496
Laundry and cleaning	315	27
Clothing	600	50
Vacation	1 500	125
Recreation & entertainment	1 800	150
Reading	200	17
Personal care	600	50
Medical/dental (not insured)	400	33
Life insurance premiums	162	13
Automobiles: John	3 454	287
Mary	3 454	287
Gifts and donations	300	25
Miscellaneous	2 050	171
TOTAL	**$33 618**	**$2 801**

10
HOW TO INCREASE YOUR
RETIREMENT INCOME

Retirement means the loss of your earnings from employment, and it is only the rare person who has managed to arrive at retirement with as much income as he or she had while working. Many will find themselves in the position of our example, with income reduced below anticipated spending. No one wants a reduction of income or enjoys reducing expenditures, but after retirement, most people manage to work out a satisfactory compromise by making good use of their assets and adjusting their lives to fit their incomes.

a. PART-TIME EMPLOYMENT

One way to remain retired, continue to use your abilities, and to supplement your income is part-time employment. If you want to continue to work, the best time to get a job is when you are still working. Employers then think they are obtaining the skill and experience of a valuable, productive person — a few months later after retirement, they may view you as an entirely different person.

Your present employer could be the best place to start. He or she knows you and your abilities and you know the organization. This will lessen the shock of change and eliminate much of the possibility of failure associated with a new, unknown organization. Even if your employer has a policy of retirement at a specific age, there may be loopholes that enable you to continue on a temporary or part-time basis. Many employers are happy to do this as it retains a standby force of experienced people available to fill in for those ill, absent on vacation, or to provide extra help in periods of heavy volume. There may also be subsidiary organizations not subject to the same rules to which you could be transferred. Your knowledge might be of value to a supplier who would be happy to have you.

Search the daily newspaper "Help Wanted" advertisements. Many jobs, without being advertised, are filled by people who appear at the plant or office door looking for work, so make the rounds of those places you consider suitable. Others are filled by persons recommended by present employees, so tell your friends you are available and what you are seeking. Register with the local employment agencies, including those who specialize in offering temporary help.

If these sources do not provide employment, look to other organizations where your skills might be of value. Consider small employers, who may be happy to have your special experience and who may be free of obstacles such as a rigid union agreement or pension plan that often make exceptions impossible with the larger organizations.

1. Canada Employment Centre

Canada Employment is a federal government organization with one aim — to help get employers and employees together. Employers list their job vacancies and people looking for work are registered, listing the details of their skills, desires, and wages sought. Canada Employment does not charge for its service; it often functions better than it is given credit for, especially where special care that a private organization could not afford to give is required, and thus it may be particularly helpful for the older worker.

Canada Employment must meticulously obey the law and cannot discriminate against older or retired people on the basis of age. As long as they are capable and want to work, Canada Employment will try to place older people and they often succeed. Usually, younger people look for positions with opportunities for advancement and refuse those without them. Such positions are often, therefore, left for older people.

Canada Employment Centres are listed in telephone directories, under Government of Canada, Employment and Immigration.

2. Should you take training?

The common assumption that older people cannot learn has been thoroughly disproven. The question is one of motivation: *if you want to learn, you can!*

Job opportunities are most available in the areas of new skills. This is particularly true of clerical work where, for example, training to upgrade from a typist to a word processor operator or computer operator could make finding a job easier. A Canada Employment Centre counsellor can tell you where these opportunities are; sometimes organizations are willing to pay for re-training. You can also investigate courses through continuing education or trade schools.

There is a job available for you somewhere if you want it, but it is up to you to find it and convince the employer that you are the right person to do it!

3. Self-employment

There are two different possibilities under the category of self-employment. One is to be a freelancer and sell your services to all comers. You are independent, not an employee, and contract to do some specific work for an agreed price. Many organizations are happy to employ individuals in this way. It fixes their costs, eliminates hiring other employees, and does away with all the multitude of extra expenses, returns, and responsibilities that go with every name on a payroll. From your standpoint, it makes a controlled amount of part-time work possible, and there need be very little investment. The work may be done at home or on the purchaser's premises depending on circumstances. What skills do you have to offer that are related to your experience?

The second possibility is to start your own business. There is no reason why you should not, provided you have the means, knowledge, experience, and energy to do so. To operate any business, of course, you must know what you are doing if you don't want to be burned. Often, the best way is to buy an established business. It will be best if you study up and learn about it to be sure of your course. This, in itself, can be a very worthwhile undertaking, even if it never leads to more positive action. (See *Starting a Successful Business in Canada*, another title in the Self-Counsel Series.)

Many people have built very rewarding and successful businesses after retirement. It is your right to try. Good luck!

4. Executives and professionals

Often, professionals belong to associations. If your specialty has one, you will know about it. This is the place to start as most possible openings will be known to them. They would perhaps be able to advise about the possibility of selling your services as a consultant. Prepare a proper resume of your training and experience, and state the kind of work you seek and the remuneration desired. Mail it to possible prospects, including placement agencies. Make phone calls to acquaintances and ask for suggestions.

b. MAKE YOUR ASSETS EARN MORE INCOME

You can also increase your income by rearranging all your present assets so that you will perhaps have both a greater income and a better life. You have spent a lifetime acquiring these assets. Now use them to the best possible advantage. This may mean exchanging one home for another, changing your transportation habits, rearranging your investments and life insurance, and perhaps revising your spending patterns.

To increase the income from all those things, start by considering how your assets are employed, examining each carefully. Does each produce money income or, if it does not, does it provide satisfaction worth the value of the income it replaces? Look at your cash, investments, home, insurance and cottage to see if you are getting as much out of them as you should. How little income is earned by a considerable sum of valuable items may surprise you!

You may not realize how much you have accumulated in total assets during your career. Most of these assets were not obtained originally to produce income; often their accumulation was a byproduct of some other enterprise. Do you know how much they total? Have you calculated how this sum could increase your income if rearranged and invested for this purpose?

Find what you have to work with by listing the value of all your assets. Separate those belonging to husband and wife because this may be important when planning for your taxes.

Follow this checklist and put down a dollar value for each item:

Cash
Bank account
Life insurance cash value
Life insurance accumulated dividends
Stocks, bonds, and investments
Art objects and antiques
Investment property
Value of house
Value of cottage
Automobile
Other

Now you have a figure to work with: the money you would have if you sold everything and put the cash into a bank account.

Suppose that you moved back home from residence in a foreign country and had this sum of cash to use to set up your home, investments, and life here and could make a completely new start. Would you choose the home and the location you have now, the clubs, cottage, furnishings, investments, and would you buy the same insurance policies if you had the opportunity to do so?

If your answer is no, you are free to convert almost all of these assets into cash and buy what you wish now. The only exception might be your life insurance as it might not be replaceable. Consider any change there carefully after reading the later discussion of this asset.

When deciding whether to buy or rent a home, you must balance the satisfaction derived from the alternatives. Think of the uses for investment income should you choose to rent or purchase a less expensive home.

If you decide to cash the assets and invest the total, how much income will it bring? The rates of interest usually vary considerably over a year, but at the time of writing, bank and trust company certificates bring around 7%. These are considered secure and most are guaranteed by the Canada Deposit Insurance Corporation for up to $60 000 for each investor. If you have more than this, it can be spread by purchasing from different companies.

To know what investment income could be generated, multiply the total value by the current rate of interest and divide by 100. (This means multiply by the rate of interest and knock off the last two figures on the right.) If you wish, you need not spend any of your capital. You could invest it all and use the income to rent almost everything you require.

c. BANKING FACILITIES

1. Cash and chequing accounts

First, let us consider how to handle your cash. This is normally kept in bank, trust company, or credit union accounts. It is there to serve two purposes: as a reserve of money available to pay regular and perhaps unexpected expenses and to generate as much interest income as possible.

For most efficient use, establish what you require for regular monthly expenses and keep one account for this purpose. Next, scrape all other cash sources together and look for maximum investment income from it. About half the investment income earned by retired people comes from account interest so do not neglect it.

There are three recent innovations in accounts offered by banks, trust companies, credit unions, or caisses populaire that can reduce costs and greatly increase income. The first is the daily calculation of interest on the account balance. As account balances can fluctuate widely, the daily interest account can earn you much more interest.

The second is that most organizations now eliminate charges for cheques, payment of utility bills, and issuing money orders or travellers' cheques for people over 60.

The third is that while interest rates were greatly reduced in 1992, there are still many options which may help offset this decline. At the time of writing, there is a wide range of accounts offered by banks and trust companies with rates ranging from 0% to 3%. Term deposits for 60 to 90 days earn 3.75%; for a one-year term deposit banks will pay 5.5% and trust companies 6%. These rates may be as high or higher than you earned before the drop.

If John and Mary decide that they could tie up $5 000 for one year, their earned interest could be increased by $150.

Use only those banks and trust companies that are members of the Canada Deposit Insurance Corporation and that can insure each person for up to $60 000 in each member organization used. In the case of credit unions or caisses populaire, use only those insured by provincial organizations.

2. Credit cards

Credit cards are convenient and can actually earn you money by deferring payment for purchases if you pay off your account in full each month. Some cards charge for their services, others do not, so choose one of the latter. All charge a high rate of interest if the account is not paid when due. There may be no charge provided payment is made by the prescribed date. The time lag between purchase and payment, often two months, leaves this money with you to earn interest for that time. If there are "specials" where such credit cards cannot be used, it is generally best to pay cash to take advantage of them.

3. Guaranteed investment certificates

While you are investigating various types of accounts, ask about the branch's investment certificates or certificates of deposit and debentures or whatever name each has for longer-term, fixed income investments. Ascertain the following facts:

(a) What lengths of contract are available (for example, one to five years)?

(b) What is the rate of interest for each?

(c) Can they be cashed on request before maturity? (This is important.) Is there a penalty in interest for doing so?

(d) Can these certificates be sold or assigned as security? (Some cannot.) If so, and the money is needed before maturity, can the debenture be sold? (Some cannot.) There may be a small discount, but at least the funds are available when needed. Often the bank or trust company manager can sell them for you or they can be sold through a regular bond dealer or privately to a friend.

(e) Can interest be paid monthly?

(f) Will the company redeem them without penalty, if requested, upon the owner's death?

(g) Are they protected by government deposit insurance?

4. Canada Savings Bonds

Canada Savings Bonds are ideal investments for retired people. They can be cashed at once over the counter at all banks and trust companies. They are guaranteed by the Government of Canada, and the interest rate is often about 3% above account interest rates.

The annual rate of interest is changed November 1 of each year. The same rate applies to both outstanding bonds and the new issue. Bonds issued prior to 1987 have a set minimum and the new rate cannot be below it. The rate is often increased upward during the year if other interest rates rise above the minimum being paid on the bonds. Interest is paid only once a year, in November.

You may want to consider dividing purchases into several units so that only a part need be cashed if money is required.

5. Money market funds

Money market funds are a relatively new type of daily interest account operated by financial houses. They are not suitable for small sums but useful for holding sizable fluctuating balances, which must be readily available, earning more than bank interest. Rates vary but usually are between bank account rates and longer term certificate rates. They are usually nonchequing but funds are available on demand. Look into the investment policies and insurance backing of any considered.

6. Summary

With this information, you are ready to decide where you will do your banking. Remember that it is wise for you to have some assets that can be readily converted into cash to meet emergencies in health, housing repairs, etc. To maximize your earnings and decrease your expenses, take the following steps:

(a) Use banking facilities as described above.

(b) To be ready for major emergencies or other substantial cash requirements, hold the amount you think you might require in securities which can be cashed at will without capital loss, such as Canada Savings Bonds or cashable bank or trust company certificates.

(c) Put the balance in some high-yielding secure investments, preferably those that can be sold or assigned at will.

d. A PREARRANGED INSTANT LOAN

It is convenient to assign some assets to your bank or trust company as security so you can issue a cheque at home or abroad for more than the cash in your account and up to the value of the security. Arrange with the manager that if you issue such a cheque, it will never be refused because the bank will automatically create a loan against your security and deposit it in your account to cover the cheque. (Loans against good securities are made at a lower rate of interest, too!)

This serves two purposes: supplying a convenient source of funds when quickly required and making these funds available without selling the security. The funds may be required only for a short time, and it is more economical to pay the interest than to sell the security and then reinvest when the funds are available again. If the requirement is permanent and securities must be liquidated, time is provided to decide on the best course instead of forcing an ill-considered action.

Before borrowing money, you should realize that the cost or interest rate will vary considerably depending on the organization from which you borrow and the security you give. If you go to a bank or trust company and borrow against government bonds or their own certificate, you will get the lowest rate. It will pay you to investigate and take advantage of the best opportunity.

e. HOW TO MAKE YOUR LIFE INSURANCE PRODUCE INCOME NOW

You bought life insurance in the first place to protect your family. The most important decision now is whether to terminate the policy and invest the cash value or to keep it in force but take advantage of its provisions to earn income. Many do not realize that this can be done. Which is the better course will depend on your personal circumstances and, as the provisions of policies vary greatly, on the terms of your particular policy.

Is there someone for whom you should maintain all the financial protection possible if you die first? How important is current income compared with that future protection? Will a compromise that keeps the insurance in force and provides some income now be enough to cover your needs?

You have already determined your need for extra income; now consider the necessity of providing for any responsibility you may have for a spouse, relative, or disabled child. Balance one factor against the other to reach a decision.

When you bought your insurance some years ago, you had a choice of many types of policies. If the sales person suggested that you buy standard insurance rather than "term," he or she probably pointed out certain possible future advantages of doing so. Whole life policies build up an ever-increasing cash surrender value (C.S.V.) over the years while term policies do not. The C.S.V. can be drawn as cash, used as security for a loan, used to purchase paid-up insurance, or turned into an annuity.

You have paid a higher premium to build up this C.S.V.; it is a form of saving and this money is yours. Use it wisely now and it can transform your insurance from an expense into a source of income. To be sure that you know what your policy provides, read it now. It is a legal contract and sets out in detail exactly what it will do for you. The more common policies and their features are as follows.

1. Term insurance

Term insurance is written for a specific number of years: 5, 10, or 15, or perhaps until a certain age, then it terminates. You have no insurance beyond that date and it very rarely goes beyond 65 years of age. It has no cash surrender value, but most term policies contain the right to change them into standard policies at the going rate for your age and sex without medical examination, up to a certain date.

2. Endowment policy

An endowment policy is written to terminate at a certain date at which point the face value is paid to the beneficiary and no further premiums are payable. It is usually written to provide a sum of money at a certain age for a specific purpose, such as a college education, a home, or retirement.

3. Whole life insurance

Whole life insurance will carry on until death, at which time the face value of the policy plus any dividends that have accumulated and less any loans against it will be paid to the beneficiary. One of the problems now is that you continue to pay the same premiums all through retirement. This is one of the expenses that you may be able to eliminate, but if it is a participating policy, the dividends it pays may be used to substantially reduce the cost of carrying it (see Sample #6 where the annual premium is $163, the dividend $156 and the cost $7 in the 38th year).

4. Life insurance with premiums payable for a specified term

These policies are generally referred to as "20 pay," "30 pay," life or any other specified term of years, which means that you pay premiums for that number of years only. The policy then continues in force until death or until some other option is exercised.

5. Participating insurance

Participating insurance means that the policy participates and shares in the company's earnings and you receive your share through policy dividends, usually allotted annually. You can elect to have those dividends accumulate and the company pay interest on the accumulated value, or you can draw them as cash or have them deducted from the annual premium payable to reduce it. While term insurance generally earns dividends, these usually must be drawn annually and not accumulated.

The annual dividend for a participating policy will not be shown in any policy as it is not a guaranteed feature. Its amount is not known until the company has calculated its profits and decided on the amount pay

131

able each year. You will, therefore, receive an annual statement showing the dividend allotted for the year plus any accumulation from prior years.

If you have permitted dividends to accumulate, there is only one recommended course: draw them now and invest the money in secure investments such as those previously discussed. They will probably earn more interest than paid by the insurance company.

6. Non-participating insurance

A non-participating insurance policy, in contrast to the previous one, does not participate in the company's profits and earns no dividends.

7. Your options

Every policy other than term will show a cash surrender value for specified dates over the life of the policy. If it does not show one for the approximate date on which you are examining the policy, the company will provide this for you on request. The C.S.V. is the amount that is payable if the policy is cancelled and no longer exists as insurance. This can be done at any time and you can do whatever you wish with the money.

When there is a C.S.V., the following options are usually available.

(a) Terminate the policy and take the C.S.V. in cash. Part of the C.S.V. may be classed as income and must be added to your current income when computing income tax. Ask your insurance company if part of your C.S.V. is so classed before taking action.

(b) Your present policy can be exchanged for a paid-up policy of a lower face value without your having to pay further premiums. The size of the new policy will depend on your age at the date of exchange and will be shown in the policy. Check to see if you have the option of a participating or non-participating policy. In the example in Sample #6, a $10 000 policy can be exchanged for a new $7 570 paid-up participating policy. In this case, the insured retains a policy of about 75% of the original. No further premiums are payable and, as it is a participating policy, annual dividends of about $100 per year might be available after the first year.

(c) The policy can be terminated and the C.S.V. used to buy an annuity. The policy sets the prices at which the company guarantees to sell you certain types of annuities. This is of very little value in most cases today because the old cost of annuity is much higher than the current one and you would probably be unwise to purchase at the prices shown. Therefore, the company will usually sell you an annuity at a lower price than that specified so, if you wish to consider one, ask for the current rates. Obtain competitive rates and buy from the best source.

(d) Borrow the cash surrender value and invest it at a profit. It is not necessary to cancel the policy to use the C.S.V. to earn an income. A policy usually specifies that the policy holder can demand a loan of the cash surrender value of the policy, less one year's interest payments. The rate of interest to be charged is set and, in many of the older policies, it may be 6%. This means that the C.S.V. could be borrowed at 6% and reinvested at the going interest rate.

If invested to earn income, the cost of borrowing is usually deductible from taxable income.

Keep records to verify how the borrowed money was invested.

This, together with the annual dividend, would enable you to still carry your insurance in force, retaining it for your spouse, dependants, or heirs. Instead of the expense of paying the premiums out of income, it would provide a net cash profit for current spending!

(e) Terminate the policy and leave the C.S.V. on deposit at interest with the company. As the rate of interest is usually well below other secure alternatives, this is probably not a wise course.

The first decision to make is whether you wish to retain the insurance or surrender it and take the C.S.V. If the latter, the C.S.V. may be treated like any other capital; use it to buy an annuity from the insurer, or from another company if you can obtain a better rate elsewhere. Shop around, for there is often considerable difference in rates and you have every right to do so. It is not necessary to buy an annuity, and some of the alternatives will be considered later.

8. An important decision

If you have life insurance, you must now make an important decision regarding the policy, but only after careful consideration and with a full understanding of the facts. Once made, it may be final, and you can't change your mind. Don't let one person, particularly someone who stands to gain from a favorable decision, talk you into some course of action. Look into the alternatives and discuss them with your spouse and trusted advisors.

Balance the facts. Protect those for whom the insurance was purchased to protect, and then use it to give the balance of present income and future increase in your estate which you consider desirable.

WHOLE LIFE PARTICIPATING INSURANCE

Face value: $10 000.00
Date: 38 years after date of issue
Annual premium: $163.20
Net premium cost: $7.20 after deducting dividend
Options:

1. Exchange for a paid-up participating policy worth
    $7 570 and receive an annual dividend estimated
    at $100.

2. Surrender the policy for $5 330 C.S.V. and invest
    the money or purchase an annuity which would
    purchase a joint annuity, guaranteed 10 years,
    starting at age 65, of $498 per annum or $41.57
    per month.

3. Borrow $5 010 against C.S.V. at 6% and reinvest
    at a higher current rate.

4. If dividends have been allowed to accumulate,
    withdraw the total amount of $5 738 now and
    if invested at 6% would yield $344 per annum.
    If combined with the $5 330 cash surrender value
    and used to buy an annuity as above, it would
    provide an annual income of $1 037.

Results of various options listed above
1.Take a paid-up participating policy.
    (a) Premiums are no longer payable.
    (b) A dividend income of, perhaps, $100.00
    (c) An insurance of $7 570.00 remains in force.

---

2. Surrender policy and take C.S.V.

   (a) Invested at 6% yields $344 per annum. Annuity as above yields $498.

   (b) No further life insurance is in force.

3. Borrow and invest C.S.V.

   (a) Cost of borrowing $5 010.00
   at 6% $300.60
   Add cost of annual premium $163.20
   Total $463.80

   Subtract reduction in costs
   by annual dividend $156.00
   Combined cost of policy and loan $307.80

   (b) Investing the borrowed $5 010

   at 8% yields an income of $400.80
   at a cost, as in (a), of $307.80
   Profit $ 93.00

   (c) Insurance of $10 000 remains in force and, as long as it does, the C.S.V. will increase by approximately $169.00 per year. Remember, on your death, any loan outstanding will be deducted from the face value of the policy when paid, but the investment should be available as an off-setting factor.

Check your policy to see who your beneficiary is; if in doubt, ask the company to confirm this for you. This is important, for the company must pay the proceeds to the named beneficiary on the death of the insured. It often happens that the insured names some specific person, such as a parent, relative, or spouse when the policy is taken out and then forgets about it. The years pass and relationships change. The insured then thinks that the insurance is part of his or her estate but instead it goes to the named beneficiary who may have died or become a divorced spouse or to someone for whom the insured no longer wishes to provide. Be sure that the beneficiary in your policy is correctly shown.

f.   SHOULD YOU LIVE ON CAPITAL?

Most retired people must spend capital to maintain their standard of living. Often the difference between capital and interest is not understood. A good illustration is the goose and the golden eggs she laid: the goose being the capital, the eggs being the interest. Once the goose is gone, there are no more eggs. It is important to know what your capital is and if you are spending it or just the interest from it. You can easily differentiate them by putting the income into an investment or a savings account. Then the interest or dividend earned will become obvious.

It may be desirable for you to spend capital, but you should understand what you are doing and be certain that it will not create a future problem. You may not need to spend capital regularly but may do so from time to time for large purchases or in emergencies. You may choose to dispose of non-income-producing items as suggested in the previous chapter (your children may not value them anyway) or you may need to sell income-producing assets and thereby eat the goose that lays the golden eggs.

If you plan to sell a capital asset, ascertain your possible capital gains tax liability before doing so. As there are different methods of determining how much, if any, is taxable capital gain, have a knowledgeable person advise you. If you have a choice of assets, you may find that those of equal value will attract different amounts of tax, usually because of the changes in their values since valuation day (at the end of 1971). This applies to almost any asset valued at $1 000 or over with the exception of your principal residence. Under a recently introduced provision, most capital gains up to a lifetime total of $100 000 are exempt from taxation.

g. ANNUITIES

When spending capital, the problem is to know how much can be spent each year so that it will not run out during your lifetime. The answer would be simple if you knew when your life would end, but without this information you have the choice of reducing the annual expenditure to the point where it will continue to the end of the longest possible expected life, or to arbitrarily select some earlier date and hope that life will not extend beyond it.

The predicament can be readily solved by the purchase of an annuity, for the companies who sell them resolve the problem by pooling many lives, calculating the average length, and then collecting sufficient premiums which, together with the interest it will earn before distribution, will pay each participant a guaranteed amount for life.

Many different kinds of annuities are available. Purchasers take a calculated gamble; those who live short lives get a relatively poor return; those who live long lives hit the jackpot and receive a much greater return. Annuities are popular because no one knows to which group he or she will belong, and although one gamble is involved, another is eliminated — the risk of the well running dry before life ends.

1. Poor health, lower cost

Insurers may sell a given annuity for less to persons with poor health. If you do have a health problem and intend to buy an annuity, it is to your advantage to disclose this fact. If the issuing company feels that your health is likely to create a shorter life expectancy than average, it may give you a greater annual income for the same purchase price. This is an additional reason to obtain a quotation from several companies, as their options for your disability may differ.

An annuity is any periodic payment. It is a legal contract that defines what it will do, and there are several types available. You may purchase one in advance of the starting date by contracting to make certain payments from that time until the date the annuity begins or you can purchase one for a lump sum in advance or at the time commencement is desired.

Most life insurance policies specify that at death the beneficiary may take the proceeds as an annuity if desired. They also have tables showing how much of different types of annuity can be purchased for every $1 000 available from the policy. The following are the common types of full life or joint annuities.

(a) Life annuity pays an agreed sum at stated intervals for life of the annuitant.

(b) Joint annuity pays the annuitant and, in the event of his or her death, the joint annuitant (perhaps the spouse) for the rest of his or her life, should he or she survive the original annuitant. It may be arranged to have the survivor paid the same or a lesser sum.

(c) Term certain annuity pays the annuitant for life or a specified number of years, starting from the date of initial payout, whichever is longer (often 15 years). Should death occur before the specified number of years has elapsed, the annuity continues to pay some other designated person the regular payments until the end of the term.

(d) There are escalating annuities in which the payments increase annually. At the start of the plan, payment for a certain sum invested would be lower than that from a regular annuity, but the increasing payments would be greater in a few years. Many of the plans increase payments by 4% per year. For example, if the payments started out at $65.12 per month in an escalating annuity, they would be increased by the fifth year to pay $76.18 a month, in the tenth year to $92.67, and by the fifteenth year, the payments would be $112.74 per month. The same investment in a standard joint annuity (ten year minimum payments) might pay $91.41. Which would yield the most in total depends on the ages the annuitant and spouse reach. Which is most desirable in other respects is a personal decision.

(e) One type of annuity that is gaining in popularity is the Registered Retirement Income Fund (RRIF), which is explained in chapter 12.

An alternative to spending your capital or buying an annuity is to invest it safely at as high a rate of interest as possible and spend only the interest earned. At today's high yields it is possible to earn as high a rate of return in this manner as you would receive from purchasing an annuity. Federal and provincial government bonds can be purchased to provide the same return on your investment, or better.

If the annuity is chosen, on the completion of its term all the capital will be gone; if the bonds are chosen, the capital will remain intact and can be willed to heirs or charities. Why, then, do so many favor annuities?

There is the convenience, for the company does the investing, but your capital is given in payment for the company's service. Some dislike the responsibility of investing and are afraid of the problem of reinvesting. There are, for example, provincial government guaranteed bonds paying over 10%, which run until after the year 2000, over 20 years.

There may be a difference in income tax paid. The total of annuity payments received in a year is not always subject to tax. This is not because the rate is actually lower, but because part of the amount of the cheques is just a return of capital and, therefore, not taxable; the entire bond interest is. The difference is that some annuities are purchased with saved money on which income tax has been paid. This is so with the income from those purchased with insurance policy proceeds, while the income from an annuity bought out of registered retirement savings plans would be fully taxable.

2. A comparison of annuities

The size of the monthly payment per dollar invested will vary with —

(a) the kind of contract chosen,

(b) the interest rates at date of purchase, and

(c) the individual company's decision for rates on that date.

Monthly payments could be lower with lower interest rates and higher with higher rates.

h. ART OBJECTS AND ANTIQUES

You may be surprised how much some of the things you own are worth, so don't dispose of them without determining their value. How often have you walked by an antique shop and seen old crockery, equipment, and furniture displayed at substantial prices and similar to something you or your family threw out not so long ago? Even items you know to be valuable may have increased more than you realize.

How about those pictures? Who is the artist? One man discovered three paintings by one of the "Group of Seven" artists in his family's basement!

You have two alternatives if you have old items that have become valuable: sell them and invest the proceeds, or hold them and let them continue to increase in value. Your decision will probably depend on your present need for cash compared with your hope of obtaining a higher value in the future.

i. YOUR HOUSE OR COTTAGE

If you own a house and/or a cottage (and a condominium or co-op apartment would be included in this classification), these are probably the most valuable assets you have. Look at each one separately. They were perhaps purchased some time ago to fill a very different need. They may have been bought when you had children living at home. Is your home suitable for you now in retirement, or would you be better served with another? Perhaps your house is too big, has a high cash value, expensive taxes, heat, and maintenance. Something different might be more suitable today; should you consider making a move?

Alternative types of housing suitable for retired people are discussed thoroughly in chapter 14; however, the basic economics are considered here.

Most people, by the time they retire, have paid off the mortgage on the family home. While values of houses will vary widely with the location and type of individual home, they will be relative to others in the same area. In other words, a larger home will be much more valuable than a comparable smaller one in the same district and, if houses sell at lower prices in your area, apartments will also be rented at lower prices.

If, for example, your home will sell for $150 000, the real estate commission, legal fees, taxes, moving costs, and necessary purchases for your new home will probably cost about $10 000, leaving $140 000. At an investment rate of 10%, this will produce $14 000 in income. (When selling the house, it is probable that you will be given the opportunity of taking a first or second mortgage which would yield perhaps 4% to 6% more than the interest you would receive from the bank. You may choose to take either of these if you plan to invest the money. If you do so it may make it easier to sell the house, and may make it possible to get a higher price.) The cost of operating this home will also go with it to the new purchaser, so you will save the $4 550 operating costs.

If, however, you like your house and the neighborhood and would prefer to remain, but you have too much space, perhaps you can turn this disadvantage into a source of revenue and continue to live there. The simplest possibility is to take in boarders or rent rooms, but if you wish to go further have an architect or builder look it over. You may remodel and come out with a duplex, providing ideal accommodation for you as well as a rentable apartment to produce the extra revenue you desire. Before going too far, check the local building restrictions to see if this is permissible.

If you do not have the ready cash to pay for alterations, this would be an excellent use for any accumulated insurance dividends or a policy loan. Some provinces guarantee low-rate bank loans for this purpose and municipalities often give special tax treatment. If it looks like an acceptable possibility, look into it. Your bank manager will know the details of special loans available.

As a fringe benefit, you might be able to rent to a younger person who could look after the snow clearing, gardening, etc., and be a built-in helper when needed.

What are your alternatives?

(a) Rent an apartment at, say, $4 800 per annum. This would leave you with your accommodation paid and more income than you had before.

(b) Buy a condominium or co-op apartment.

(c) Buy a mobile home.

(d) Buy a smaller house. Here the savings would depend on your success in buying one at a sufficiently lower price to leave an important cash difference after everything is paid and on the lower operating costs of a smaller place. The most likely worthwhile difference would occur if you moved from an expensive city area to a town where the costs of the property, taxes, and maintenance are lower. Such a move could make a significant contribution to your income and ease the strain.

Your cottage can be regarded in exactly the same manner. However, a cottage has an additional advantage because, if you desire, it can be rented for part of the season and used by you for the balance of the time. The rent might pay for the carrying costs and be all the assistance you require. If owning a cottage gives you a lot of satisfaction, it's your right to try to arrange your affairs so that you can keep it. On the other hand, its sale might provide a substantial investment income which could mean a lot to you now. Such income might provide you both with a resort holiday or a trip you would enjoy and still leave some cash for other uses. Look into it and come up with the decision that is most advantageous to you and your spouse.

j. WHAT SHOULD YOU DO?

When you made your initial list of expected post-retirement income and expenses, you found either adequate income to continue or a shortage. After examining various possible changes on the income side through reusing the assets you have, you are now in a position to make a decision.

You can attack from either the income or the expenditure side, or a combination of both. Now you have the knowledge of what can be done by reusing your assets for better financial return. Perhaps you see changes that you want to make on the income side and that will solve any financial problem. If so, well and good. If not, there is still the other side.

Consider each expenditure. Is it worth it now? Would you derive greater satisfaction if the money were spent in another way? Even if not a necessity, an examination might result in more satisfaction. Later on, after you have given more consideration to the use of time, you will probably revise your decisions. Don't make a final move until all factors have been carefully considered as suggested in chapters 14 and 15.

You may decide to implement only enough of the above suggestions to provide the income change you require. On the other hand, you may choose to implement them all and enjoy extensive travelling or a winter vacation. The choice is yours.

See Sample #7 for an example of a revised plan. Before making their decision, the Joneses wish to look into the possible problems if high inflation continues. They also want to look into the various annuities and RRIFs currently available from several sources. They have decided to defer their decision until both investigations have been completed.

REVISING POSSIBLE RETIREMENT INCOME BY REARRANGING ASSETS

Life insurance
If you draw the accumulated dividends of $5 738.00 and invest it at 7%, you would have an income of $401.

Cash surrender value
By borrowing $5 010.00 against C.S.V. at 6% and reinvesting at 7%, your net income would be $50.10.

Note: Certain portions of the cash surrender value may be subject to taxation if cashed during the insured's lifetime. Ask the insurance company to tell you if there is such a liability on your policy, and how much it is.

Cancellation of insurance policy
If you cancel the policy, take the C.S.V. of $5 330.00 and invest at 7%, your annual income would be $323.00 plus your saving of $7.20 on the premium, giving a total of $330.20.

Joint annuity
If you buy a joint annuity yielding $507 per annum, the premium saved would be $7.20, totalling $514.20.

Sale of automobile and investment

Income from investing $1 500 at 7%	$ 105
Add operating costs (as per budget)	3 456
Total	$3 561
Subtract cost of public transportation	350
Net saving	$3 211

House

Sale price	$150 000
Selling expenses	10 000
Net	$140 000
Invest in government bond at 8%	11 200
Operating cost less rent	425
Total increase	$11 625

Or

Invest in joint annuity	$13 272
Operating less rent	425
Total increase	$13 697

The total possible increase in income over expenses if you carried out the suggestions above could be as follows:

Income from cashing life insurance policy and investing proceeds	$ 330
Saving in net annual insurance premiums	7
Giving up car for public transportation	3 211
Selling home, buying the annuity	13 697
Possible increase in income	$17 245

11
COPING WITH INFLATION

a. PROBLEMS: THE SQUEEZE CONTINUES

The year 1992 was a turning point for the retired. Individuals were affected differently, depending on their circumstances. The declining inflation rate reduced the rate of devaluation of reduced incomes. Declining interest rates meant that deposit income declined and that terminating or new investments were placed at lower rates.

There was an ominous admission by all levels of government: continuous borrowing to pay for services is nearing its end and the cost of services must be reduced. This has and will result in discontinuing some free services and by one means or another transferring the cost down to another level of government where the individual will pay for it directly or indirectly. At the same time, taxes and fees are being increased. These combined factors come down on individuals in the form of lower incomes and higher costs and it is probable that the trend will continue.

Those retired persons who have been relying on income from sources that fluctuate and others with maturing investments may have lower incomes. Those facing retirement may have to reevaluate their lifestyles to accommodate the above realities.

b. INVESTMENT AND BUDGETING STRATEGIES TO COUNTER INFLATION

What will the future bring? No one knows for sure. In our troubled times there is no agreement among those in the best position to know, so what do you do? Inflation and interest rates rise and fall together. If you think long-term rates will rise it would be best to defer making investments that, once committed, cannot be changed. However, if you expect rates to fall, it is best to make such investments at once. All you can do is seek good advice, understand the options available, and make a wise decision.

Once you've decided, you are then in a position to determine what your retirement income will be and you can set up a plan to live within your means. This is a most important step; attempting to live beyond your means can only result in misery.

There is good cause that there will be continuing inflation, rising in good times and falling in recessions. In ten years, at a rate of 2%, it would take $1.22 to buy what $1.00 buys today. At 4% it will take $1.48, almost one half as much again, and in 18 years, today's dollar would be worth only 50¢. If you accept this premise it would be wise to be prepared. To do so may mean a lower level of income in the beginning, but if prices rise you could be prepared with a rising level of income to meet them. If prices do not rise you will have a surplus to spend as you wish.

Old Age Security and Canada Pension Plan are indexed to keep up with inflation, so this is one part of your income that is ready to help. Here are three other suggestions:

(a) Save a part of your income for a rainy day.

(b) Plan your expenditures in such a way that if need be, the least important things, which may not have contributed greatly to your happiness, could be dropped.

(c) Consider investing in increasing annuities or an RRIF (see chapter 12).

c. GOVERNMENT ACCEPTANCE OF RESPONSIBILITY

Our governments on all levels have recognized the seriousness of inflation and are helping in a constructive way. Their actions and words indicate that they accept the responsibility to help the retired cope. In effect, these governments are providing a hedge against inflation, at least insofar as the income that they provide is concerned. Such provisions, making payments flexible in relation to a known index such as the cost of living is called indexing, a term you will hear frequently and should understand.

d. GOVERNMENT PAYMENT OF CERTAIN EXPENSES

Government-sponsored medical and hospital plans are also of great importance to the retired community. At one time, serious illness could lead to heavy expenses often resulting in a crippling financial situation. Now this has changed. Medical costs have gone up drastically, but the great financial fear they once held for the senior citizen has largely vanished with provincial hospital and medical plans. In addition, many provinces now either pay for, or assist by partial payment of many prescription drugs.

e. HOW THE OLD AGE SECURITY, CANADA, AND QUEBEC PENSIONS INCREASE

The Old Age Security Pension is reviewed quarterly; if the Consumer Price Index rises, the Old Age Security Pension is increased by the same percentage.

While it is not necessary to go into the mechanics by which the Canada Pension Plan is calculated, suffice to say that the starting pension is now increasing much more rapidly and will continue to do so because of the cumulative effect of the recent large increases in the "maximum pensionable earnings." When the plan was introduced in 1966, the maximum annual pension planned for those retiring on January 1, 1976 was expected to be $1 250 but the escalation provisions have increased this to $7 633 for 1992.

A retired person who draws a Canada Pension will have it increased annually. The percentage increase in the cost of living from November to October over the similar period 12 months earlier is added to the pension cheques for the next year, starting in January.

Realize what this means. In the past, those on fixed incomes *were* on fixed incomes. Once a pension was set, it didn't change. Prices might rise but income did not. This was the real problem. Now these pensions need no longer be classed as fixed income.

If both spouses qualify for the Old Age Security Pension and one for the maximum Canada Pension, in 1992, the two in combination would draw a total of $1 387 monthly with continued indexing.

Complaints that the increased cost of living gobbles up all pension increases are frequently heard, as if the

152

pension increase should exceed the cost of living increase. Anyone making this complaint has missed the point and unknowingly commented on the accuracy of the index, for its purpose is simply to provide enough extra income to meet the increased living costs. For those whose incomes are below the prescribed figure, there is the possibility of an additional Guaranteed Income Supplement, plus other provincial benefits.

f. YOUR PART IN HANDLING CHANGING INTEREST RATES

The Old Age Security, Canada and Quebec Pensions, and, often, employment-related pensions were made for you, not by you. But, there are many things you do control, as discussed in the previous two chapters. *Making the best of the opportunities discussed is the first, and for many the only, thing they need to do.* However, people with new money to invest, perhaps from an RRSP or retiring allowance, must decide what to do with it. In addition, previously made investments may mature or should be changed.

The best investment often depends on which way interest rates are expected to go in the future, a most difficult thing to guess. No doubt they will fluctuate as they have always done, even if the basic trend is up or down. Perhaps the best thing to do is to make an investment with which you will be satisfied regardless of which way interest rates go.

You do know certain things on which to base a decision:

(a) Rates paid on deposits may change quickly, moving up or down with basic interest rates, usually related to the Bank of Canada's "bank rate."

(b) Certain contractual obligations, such as bonds and GICs, have a stipulated interest rate that will be paid as specified until the maturity date.

(c) Other investments, such as common stocks, pay a dividend that the directors set periodically, which may remain the same as last time, be omitted, or raised. There are also "floating rate" securities that pay a rate related to the bank rate and rise and fall with it.

(d) Pensions and annuities usually pay at a set rate, but some employment pensions are indexed. Increasing annuities or RRIFs, which pay larger cheques every successive year, are available.

With this information, you will know what part of your income is beyond your control, what may increase or decrease, and what part of it is available for manipulation. Keep in mind that interest rates may well rise again, and at times when rates appear to be low, you may wish to keep some funds readily available to take advantage of them if they do rise.

g. WHICH INCOME MAY DECREASE?

The negative side of decreasing inflation is that interest rates drop with it, as they did in the early eighties while prices continued to rise. Interest rates on bank accounts decreased, and it was necessary to renew short-term investments, such as treasury bills and GICs, at successively lower rates. Mutual funds invested in interest-based securities may have reduced their payments.

Canada Savings Bonds issued in 1981 paid $19\frac{1}{2}$% in the first year and paid a minimum of $10\frac{1}{2}$% until maturity in 1988. The 1992 issue pays 6% until maturity.

Guaranteed investment certificates, bonds, mortgages, and other investments that have paid a fixed rate higher than current rates for years may have to be invested at a much lower rate on maturity. For example, $10 000 invested in a five-year bond or GIC in 1981 at 20% has paid $2 000 per annum during this period. But on maturity in 1986, the same $10 000, when reinvested at the 10¾% rate then available, yielded only $1 075 per annum during the next period. In November, 1992, it would have shrunk to $600 to $700.

h. INVESTMENTS

Perhaps the best way is to know what your expected living costs will be and then to set up a long-term, secure investment plan that will provide sufficient income to cover them. This may require reductions in your living plans, but it is most important that your costs be covered.

You can increase income and value by judicious investment, but it is a two-way street, for losses are just as possible as increases. *At this stage, safety of your investment must be the most important consideration and you should only risk funds that could be lost without serious consequences. A younger person has time to make up losses; you do not.*

It may be that keeping money in bank accounts, trust company certificates, or Canada Savings Bonds is best for you. But if you have the money, desire, experience, or the ability to study investment, go ahead, but move cautiously. Seek out good advice. If you still do not feel secure, perhaps it would be best to retain the services of a professional investment manager to set up and carry out a program designed for your needs.

i. LOCKING IN CURRENT RATES

Interest rates can go up or down. The government wants lower rates and will try to bring them down. The decision to be made is this: if you have money to invest, should you keep it in a bank account or some other place where it can be readily available, hoping for higher rates, or should you buy a long-term, fixed-rate investment to be certain the income from it won't go lower?

Bonds are an ideal way of doing this. Bonds are legally defined contracts, usually in denominations of $10 000. Dates of issue and repayment, as well as what security backs the loan and the rate and date of interest payments, are specified. Most bonds pay interest twice each year and the rate will not vary over the life of the contract. They can be purchased through brokers or the banks and they can be sold if desired before maturity at the current market price.

The advantages of bonds are that they are available in either short- or long-term issues and usually pay a considerably higher rate of interest than deposits, G.I.C.s or T Bills. The rate of interest is known, facilitating planning. The longer the term, the higher the interest rate.

Retired persons should avoid risk and therefore the federal and provincial bond issues are the most suitable.

Either the standard or increasing annuities guarantee a stipulated income for life. The RRIF is a different thing with much latitude in how the fund can be invested. They can be purchased with fixed lifelong benefits similar to the annuities, while others permit the owner to choose the investments from a prescribed list. These may be short-term securities with changing rates at every termination or fluctuating rates. In either, the income could vary widely over a lifetime.

j. MUTUAL FUNDS

A mutual fund is a business organization that invests other people's money in a broad range of securities. Mutual funds provide a convenient way for the small investor, or the person who wants someone else to manage his or her investments, to participate in the ownership of almost any kind of investment, be it bonds, stocks, mortgages, commodities, or money instruments. Each mutual fund share represents a small piece of many investments, and thus the owner achieves the security of diversification. It also provides a professional manager to look after the investing for those who do not wish to do so themselves.

There are two kinds of mutual funds. Closed end funds are those in which the shares have been issued, investments made, and the stock put on the market, much like a corporation. Management continues to monitor and run the fund. The shares are bought on a stock exchange.

The more common type of mutual fund is the open end fund. This fund arbitrarily divides the total net asset value into small portions it calls shares. These shares are usually valued between $5 and $15 and are calculated to the third decimal place. So, if the portfolio of a fund on a given day is valued at $1 000 000, and it has sold 100 000 shares, each share will be valued at $10. The value of the shares goes up and down as the value of the portfolio goes up and down. All money offered for investment is usually accepted. An owner who wants out for all or part of the shares can ask for redemption and get the money back in a reasonable time. The price is usually based on a published breakup formula.

The costs of selling and managing the funds vary. Some are quite high, which may detract from their value; consider this when making a selection.

There are a great many funds and all differ. Each has a specific goal such as capital gain or security of income, and each specifies how funds are invested. Some aim for high income and pay it out regularly. Others go for capital gain and there may be no income paid out, but the owner profits through the increased value of the shares when sold. If you are interested, investigate a wide range to see if there is something that meets your requirements.

Mutual funds often make much of the fact that they offer professional management, but the record of many of these managers has been poor. On the other hand, there are those who have done extremely well. While past records do not guarantee that they will continue to do as well in the future, it does show that they have had good luck or skill, or know someone who has. It is more likely that these will continue to do better in the future than those that have a poor record.

These funds also offer a convenient form of withdrawing relatively small amounts of cash. This is done by applying to the company to have a certain number of shares redeemed, often a much less costly process than selling a small lot of shares on the stock market. By the same token, investment can usually be made easily in small amounts.

Mutual funds are often reccommended for retired persons, but there is much to learn about them. Most involve costs and risks. Success depends on the ability of the manager; some do well, others lose money. Investigate carefully before investing in them.

Those considering investing in these funds would do well to obtain a copy of Pirbeck, from Pirbeck Investment Measurement Ltd., which measures the performance of many funds over the years.

k. REAL ESTATE

Almost any kind of real estate increased greatly in value over the period from 1970 to 1990. Many retired people live in homes that they purchased at the much lower prices in effect prior to 1970. Although prices dropped considerably during 1991 to 1992, today's prices are usually much above the original cost. Selling at these prices may provide enough investment income to pay for a rental apartment with a surplus left over for other uses. This has been the most important assistance available to enable retired people to enhance their retirement income to maintain their lifestyles. There are other possibilities.

One interesting prospect when you consider selling your own house is what to do with the money. If you wish to leave your home and plan to go into a rental unit, why not consider renting out the house rather than selling it? Turning the house into a duplex and renting one apartment is another idea. And, remember that if you rent the property there will be new factors affecting income taxes. Depreciation on the rented part will increase current exemption, so full taxes perhaps need not be paid on the rental income. Investigate to be sure your plans do not contravene local bylaws.

Find out about these matters if you contemplate renting. If you are not familiar with them, seek out the advice of a qualified accountant or lawyer to explain and calculate them for you. Careful thought is needed before you dispose of any property you own.

If you have undeveloped real estate and want to turn it into an income-producing asset, consider the possibility of leasing it on a basis that includes an escalation clause or an increase in the annual rental under stipulated circumstances. Much property is now leased for commercial and industrial purposes with provisions of this nature. If you have property, perhaps it would be wise to consider the possibility of leasing it on this basis rather than selling it outright.

Those who are experienced in the field of real estate take the time to study, learn, and move only after they feel secure. Have a trusted advisor check out your arithmetic. Move carefully. If you miss one or more deals that you attempt to make, don't be too disappointed! It is the best experience you can have and will enable you to confirm and clarify your thinking.

l. ART, JEWELS, ANTIQUES, COINS, AND STAMPS

Many knowledgeable people and corporations consider items in this category as one of the finest hedges. These do not produce an income and gain would only be realized through their eventual sale at a profit. You may have some such items that have become much more valuable than you realize, so do not dispose of anything that might fall into this classification without having it valued.

If you do find you have valuable personal property, you should balance the need for current cash against the possibility of getting a higher price later on when you might need it more. Perhaps you have collected these things as a hobby and would prefer to enjoy them as long as possible. At a later date a specific need, a desire for a trip, or some other expenditure might become the deciding factor in selling.

A good example of this is the husband and wife who had both been interested in antiques for years and had built up a fine collection. It was largely in the form of furniture and ornaments they furnished the home with. When the husband retired, an antique dealer visited and offered to buy the house and contents, thus providing a substantial cash sum to augment the owners' pensions. The couple's answer was no. They had an adequate income and, if inflation continued, these things would probably increase in value too. If more cash was needed at any time, they could obtain it by selling the antiques piece by piece. Now the couple are enjoying living with them and taking satisfaction from the memories of their pleasure in finding, purchasing, and often refinishing the pieces.

m. "THE HEDGE"

Inflation has been so steadily prevalent in Europe and the East for so long that people there have learned to mistrust paper money or fixed value securities and favor the ownership of tangible things like land, buildings, precious metals, gems, and art objects, which are considered a hedge. Such a hedge can be anything that is in limited supply, has a production and distribution cost, is in demand and for which the value will, hopefully, increase along with a scarcity value or the general price level. If it does so, the item can be sold for cash and its increase in value will provide the extra money to purchase as much of other commodities at the higher price as could have been bought with the cash at the time when the hedge was purchased.

If you simply held cash during the period of price rise, that cash would purchase less at the end than at the beginning. The hedge, by increasing in value as inflation progresses, is designed to prevent this.

12
THE REGISTERED RETIREMENT SAVINGS PLAN AND REGISTERED RETIREMENT INCOME FUND

Caution: Because of frequent changes, you should not act on the information in this chapter without inquiring at Tax Information, Revenue Canada (in the federal government listings of the telephone directory).

a. THE REGISTERED RETIREMENT SAVINGS PLAN

A registered retirement savings plan (RRSP) is a legal device that protects part of your income from taxation. These tax savings enable individuals to accumulate a much larger retirement fund. There are many different types, but all must be purchased from and supervised by licenced sources and the rules strictly observed to obtain the benefits.

These tax savings can be important even in the short term. A person with $30 000 earned income contributing 18% to an RRSP would defer paying tax of perhaps $2 100, depending on the provincial rate. In five years this could total over $10 000 plus interst.

1. Eligible contributions

In calculating your taxable income for 1992, you may deduct from your income each year the amount you contribute to RRSPs, subject to the following maximum limits:

(a) If you are self-employed or your employer does not have a pension plan or deferred profit sharing plan, you can contribute 18% of your 1992 earned income to a maximum of $12 500.

(b) If you are a member of a pension plan or deferred profit sharing plan, you can contribute 18% of your 1992 earned income *minus* the total of your 1992 pension adjustments and any net past service pension adjustments.

Pension adjustments are issued in respect of all employer registered pension plans and deferred profit sharing plans and are the deemed value of pension accruals in a year. Past service pension adjustments are issued when pension benefits are credited retroactively, i.e., in certain instances, employees are permitted to contribute to the employer pension plan for past service.

In view of the complex formulae required to determine the components needed to calculate the RRSP contribution limit for the 1991 tax year (and subsequent tax years), beginning in November, 1991 Revenue Canada will report to you directly your RRSP contribution limit for the year.

Here are the new maximum limits:

1993	$13 500
1994	$14 500
1995	$15 500

All RRSP contributions limits will be based on the previous years' pensionable earnings, which will eliminate the guess work of the past.

Provided you are 60 or over, both spouses may have their own separate and RRSPs.

2. Calculating earned income

For the purposes of your RRSP, earned income consists of salary, wages, net rental or business income, royalties from created works, alimony or maintenance payments made in response to a court order or written agreement, including maintenance payments from a common law spouse, less losses from business or rental properties or deductible alimony or maintenance payments. Superannuation or pension benefits, including the Old Age Security or Canada Pensions are not included.

Under proposed law, disability pension you receive in 1992 from the Canada Pension Plan (CPP) or the Quebec Pension Plan (QPP) is included in your 1992 earned income. This amount is shown in box 16 of your T4A(P) slip issued for 1992.

Proposed law also includes, in your 1992 earned income, an amount you receive in 1992 under a decree, order, or judgment of a court as a reimbursement of alimony or maintenance payments you deducted for 1992 or a previous year. Similarly, an amount you deducted for 1992 as a repayment of alimony or maintenance payments you included in your income for 1992, or a previous year, reduces your earned income.

3. Carry forward your unused contribution entitlements

Starting with the 1991 taxation year, you will be permitted to carry forward your unused RRSP contribution room for the year to future years (maximum seven years). Your unused RRSP contribution room for a year is:

- your RRSP contribution limit for that year, *less*

- any RRSP contribution for which you claimed a deduction in the year

4. Spousal RRSPs — a possible tax saving

All or a portion of your contributions may go to your spouse's RRSP regardless of whether or not your spouse has earned income, as long as your combined contributions to both plans do not exceed your personal limit. You may deduct both from your own return.

Whether you are retired or not, until 1994, you can transfer up to $6 000 each year of periodic pension income from a registered pension plan or a deferred profit sharing plan to a spousal RRSP, tax free. To take advantage of the tax saving possibilities both spouses should calculate their expected post retirement incomes years before the RRSPs are to be converted to income. The greatest possible tax saving would exist if one spouse had no taxable income and the other's was at or above the maximum at which the Old Age Security pension would be fully taxed back by the "Clawback" tax. If the spouse expecting the higher income transfers the maximum entitlement to the other's RRSP it would make no difference to the tax at the time, but when converted to an income-producing vehicle on retirement the income would be the spouse's and would be in the lowest tax bracket. If this could be carried far enough to reduce the higher income to below the "Clawback" threshold, the extra 15% tax on the Old Age Security pension would not apply (see chapter 8). The object is to have equal incomes, or at least sufficiently close so that none remains in a higher tax bracket than necessary.

When your spouse's plan is terminated, the money is considered your spouse's and is taxed accordingly. However, if the money is withdrawn within three years of making the contribution, the amount you contributed is taxed as your income rather than as your spouse's. If the money is withdrawn prior to the three-year limit, but your spouse has reached age 60, the funds may be used to purchase one of the approved investment plans and will not be taxed as your income.

5. Different plans

If you are considering an RRSP, look at a number of different types (not all are safe). Many plans exist today into which the investor has paid for some years and which are worth less than the money paid in! In these plans the money was invested in securities that dropped in value, and now are worth less than their cost. If these securities increase again in value, they may rise above cost. Clearly, you must be careful. Here are some of the things to consider.

First, find out what the administration costs are. Some have a heavy front end load, meaning that perhaps up to 10% is deducted from your investment as soon as it is made and then additional annual charges are incurred. Other funds charge an annual fee only, or have a charge for opening or terminating a fund. In both cases, there is often a minimum that may be high enough to make a small investment of this type uneconomical. At the other extreme, some trust companies and most credit unions administer a fund without annual cost provided they gain control of the investment.

Second, every fund specifies the kind of security in which it will be invested; it is here that the element of risk enters. If in common or preferred stocks, the value will fluctuate with the value of the securities. The dividends on stocks are generally lower, and there is no compensating advantage in income tax saving in an RRSP; thus these funds rely more on the possibility of capital gains for growth.

Other funds may be invested in bonds that may also fluctuate, but the higher interest rate is a much more important factor to the retired person. Others invest in mortgages which perhaps have the highest interest component. Ask about redemption policy and whether the investment is in insured mortgages or not. Administration costs are often higher and may offset the higher interest rate. A very secure type is offered by some trust companies in which the funds are placed in their own guaranteed certificates that do not fluctuate in value and that pay about as high a rate of interest as is available on sound securities. These should provide an insured progressive increase in value with the steady compounding of interest and the elimination of any capital loss, provided the company is a member of the Canada Deposit Insurance Corporation or, in the case of credit unions, is insured by a provincial plan.

Some plans are tied in with life insurance and require contractual annual payments. Only purchase such a plan with full understanding of it and after comparing it with alternatives.

6. Taking out the money

Money can be taken out of an RRSP at any time in whole or in part but keep the following in mind.

(a) Any taken out becomes part of your taxable income. If you have unused exemptions, that portion covered by them will not be taxed.

(b) Any surplus above the exemptions will be taxed unless you are 60 or over.

(c) If you are between 60 and 71, the proceeds from the terminated RRSP may be used to purchase any of the eligible investments listed below without being taxed at the time, but the transaction must conform to rigid rules.

(d) The RRSP must be terminated by the end of the year in which you turn 71.

(e) Until March, 1994 the Home Buyer's Plan will permit borrowing up to $20 000 tax free from your RRSP to help you buy or build a qualifying home. If interested, get the *Home Buyer's Plan* booklet for full information.

If the owner dies before an RRSP has been terminated, its value is added to the owner's income for that year for tax purposes unless the spouse is entitled to receive it by will or law. If so, the spouse could either —

(a) take the cash in a lump sum and include it in current income for tax purposes, or

(b) transfer the money, without paying tax, to an RRSP in his or her name.

7. Eligible investments for transfer

The money in an RRSP can be transferred (age 60 to 71) without tax to purchase any of the eligible investments listed below. If not used in this way it becomes part of taxable income in the year drawn.

These are the eligible investments:

(a) Any of the regular forms of life annuity, including joint or survivor annuities

(b) A fixed term annuity (Annuity payments are made to the annuitant, or the spouse if the annuitant dies, until the 90th birthday)

(c) A registered retirement income fund

8. The registered retirement income fund

There are major advantages and disadvantages, depending on your needs, between a life annuity and an RRIF. First, there are broad flexible rules covering the annual payment, but there is always a lower starting rate that increases annually. You can choose a plan to suit your needs, and payments in later years can be substantially higher if desired. An RRIF can also be an important source of annually increasing income and it can be cancelled at any time so you can withdraw the money remaining in the fund. RRIFs can be payable jointly, which means they can provide continuing spousal protection for life. Finally, when the beneficiaries die, the balance remaining in the fund goes to the heirs.

There are two important changes coming in 1993. First, an RRIF will continue for life instead of terminating at age 90. This is important because it is probable that almost one-third of those reaching 71 will live beyond the age of 90.

Second, the minimum starting point for an RRIF will be increased. This, coupled with the longer payout period, will reduce the rate of increase of the annual payments, the inflation off-setting feature of the previous plan. Rates of annual or monthly payments can only be determined by requesting several companies to submit plans when you are ready.

The RRIF has several advantages over the life annuity. With an annuity the monthly payments remain the same throughout its life; your money is locked in and nothing remains at the end. The RRIF is just that: a fund that remains under your control and that gives greater flexibility in selecting payout and how it is invested. It must be made from specified sources such as an RRSP. Specified minimum amounts must be withdrawn annually, subject to tax, but larger cheques may be withdrawn if desired. An RRIF can be withdrawn, tax exempt, and the funds used to purchase an annuity. Otherwise, it can be withdrawn and used as desired, but will be subject to tax. When the last beneficiary dies, the money remaining, after expenses, is returned and distributed as the owner has directed. Thus, there is considerable flexibility to meet changing circumstances and needs. If the beneficiaries do not use up the entire fund, the remainder is available for heirs.

There are several basic kinds of RRIFs, depending on how your payment is invested. For some, the size of the monthly payment is guaranteed while others, which may be based on a floating or variable interest rate, may fluctuate.

The income that can be purchased with a given sum varies from day to day because the interest rate available for investments of the funds fluctuates, and individual companies also quote widely different rates. Sometimes the company that quoted the best rate last month is the poorest today. Life insurance companies sell the annuities that cover the owner for life. Trust companies sell only those annuities that are for a fixed term to 90. It has become so complicated that when you are buying either an annuity or an RRIF, you should consult either an individual or an organization specializing in this work to have all of the options explained.

There is one other question in addition to rates of payment to investigate. If the annuitants die before the guaranteed term has been completed, the remaining obligations are valued by the issuing company and paid to the estate in a lump sum. The method of valuation varies widely from company to company, so it is a point to compare.

Note: In all transactions related to an RRIF, be certain to follow the rules. Failure to do so may make the money subject to taxation. Changes in legislation and its application are frequent, so ask your supplier for current rules before taking action.

9. How to make your decision

Of the options available for the money you take out of an RRSP, there may be one that is clearly the best choice for you. There is none that is the best for everyone; you must decide what fills your needs best. The choice would be easy if you knew how long you and your spouse were going to live and what the inflation rate was going to be.

Here are some questions to consider when making your decision. See Table #2 for the average life expectancy of your age group.

(a) Do you need as much income as possible now, or could you do with none or little now in order to have a greater one at a later date?

(b) Would you prefer to keep control of your money and invest it yourself?

(c) What is your expected rate of income tax between now and your 71st birthday?

(d) What tax will be payable if you do not buy an eligible investment from RRSP funds?

(e) After retirement, will you have some room to increase your income without reaching a taxable level? If so, the money could be taken in annual instalments up to this amount and spent or invested as desired. The tax on the balance could be deferred by putting it into an eligible investment now or later, or you might be willing to pay tax on a part of it.

(f) What will the position of your spouse or dependant be if you die first? Is continued income protection required? Do you have life insurance that would replace the income for the spouse if you took an annuity for only as long as you live?

No decision should be made which, if it turns out badly, could result in consequences too serious to be acceptable.

If you decide that you want to keep control of your capital or that you wish to leave as much as possible to heirs or a charity, you must take the money, preferably

TABLE #2
LIFE EXPECTANCY

IF YOUR CURRENT AGE IS	THEN THE AVERAGE LIFE EXPECTANCY FOR YOUR AGE GROUP IS	
	Male	Female
60	77.69	82.85
61	78.25	83.03
62	78.56	83.22
63	78.88	83.42
64	79.21	83.63
65	79.57	83.85
66	79.93	84.09
67	80.32	84.33
68	80.72	84.59
69	81.14	84.86
70	81.50	85.14

in a way to keep tax as low as possible. If you bought an annuity or one of the other options, the money would be used up during your lifetime, although under those plans that guarantee payments for a specific period, a balance may remain if you and your spouse both die before the guaranteed term has been completed.

The life annuity will pay the greatest starting income, and if you are one of those who will enjoy a long life, it will pay the greatest total income to you. Its weaknesses are that it ceases with the death of the person on whose life it was placed, there is no remaining capital, and payments do not increase with the passage of time.

The increasing annuity pays for life, and payments increase annually. But, it has the disadvantage of lower payments in early years.

The joint and survivor annuity protects both spouses for life and is thus often the safest bet for couples unless there is other provision to support a survivor. Its weaknesses are that no capital remains and payments do not increase.

The RRIF may have lower payments in the beginning and may have steadily increasing payments for life, but these are optional and will depend on how you set it up. Depending on the length of the beneficiaries' lives, there may be a lump sum remaining after the beneficiaries' deaths. Like the life annuity, it protects the beneficiaries for life.

The fixed term to age 90 has no advantages not available in other annuities, except return of remaining capital if beneficiaries do not reach 90.

It is usually a good idea to discuss these options with some person whose opinion you respect. In the end it is you who must decide which one will best fulfil the needs of you and your spouse.

Choose only secure investments or understand the risk involved when purchasing certificates from a bank, trust company, or credit union. Accept only those insured under a government program.

b. THE FINAL PLAN

With an income $22 698 and expenses of $33 618 some very extensive changes must be made, either to increase income or reduce expenses. After considering their options, the Joneses have decided that they want to keep their cottage for summer living; that was one of the benefits they looked forward to in retirement. They would like to spend the remainder of the year in the city to be near friends, family, and other interests that are important to their happiness. They like their house, but being away all summer means the garden is no longer an attraction. They decided to sell their house and find a suitable apartment to reduce their living costs and to increase income.

They found an acceptable apartment for $400 per month. The house sold for $150 000 and after paying commission and expenses they had $140 000 left for investment. Because it was their principal residence, there would be no capital gains tax to pay.

Both had worked at different addresses, so a car for each was an advantage, but after retirement one car was sufficient, a saving of $3 454 every year.

Their task now is to invest the money from the sale of the house. They will not want to take risks so will choose a safe investment with known monthly payments. It will be important to select an experienced investment counsellor who can discuss their requirements and offer sound advice. Such a person will get quotations from many companies for different kinds of annuities and RRIFs and provide detailed information about the payout year by year for each one. The counsellor should also be able to show how the dollar cost of living will increase year by year at a specified rate of inflation. This will show the income required to keep up their purchasing power. With this information the Joneses will be able to set up a comparison of cost of living with possible income (see Table #3). Then they will know which investment will generate enough income to pay for their proposed lifestyle.

There are several factors the Joneses will take into account when deciding on the type of investment that they will make. First of all, if they live the average lifespan, John will live for about 15 years and Mary for 19. They may live much longer; should they plan for their eighties and nineties?

Trying to guess if there will be inflation and how much is almost impossible. With the return of more normal conditions many expect that it will continue, but at a lower rate. They think that the government will accept perhaps 2% as an acceptable rate of inflation. Table #3 is calculated on that basis and shows the effect on the cost of living and on income.

Second, it is becoming more and more certain that Canada's deficit and debt position will force tax increases and the reduction of government services. This means that the individual will pick up the cost of providing these services and the increased tax bill.

The Joneses must decide whether inflation, increased taxes, and paying for services will increase the cost of living during their retirement years and if so, what provision should be made for it.

In Table #3, $33 618 is used as the base cost of living (see Sample #5). The changes introduced by selling the house and one of the cars reduces this to $29 587. Each column contains the following information over a 25-year period:

- **Column #1:** The John and Mary's estimated cost of living at a 2% annual increase.

- **Column #2:** The expected combined income of their OAS and CPP at a 2% annual rate of increase, plus an estimate of Canada Savings Bond and bank account interest, with the $140 000 from the sale of the house invested in a joint annuity payable as long as either John or Mary lives.

- **Column #3:** The same basic pension and interest income as above, but with the $140 000 invested in a joint annuity that increases 4% annually.

- **Column #4:** The same basic pension and interest income, but with the $140 000 invested in an RRIF from which the minimum required withdrawals are taken.

- **Column #5:** The money remaining in the RRIF's residual fund, which can be partly withdrawn at any time, or entirely, less expenses, if the RRIF is collapsed. When the last survivor dies, any money remaining in the fund, less expenses, is returned to his or her estate.

Now go ahead and make your own plan. Always keep in mind that whatever you decide now will affect your welfare for the rest of your lives; so be well informed, seek advice, and choose carefully. Go through the following steps:

(a) Make estimates of your expected income and cost of living.

(b) Review your expenditures for possible reductions.

(c) Review your investments, assets, and sources of income and work out a more suitable lifestyle that will provide you with a higher income.

TABLE #3
EFFECT OF INCOME ADJUSTMENTS OVER 25-YEAR PERIOD*

Year	1. Cost of living with 2% increase	2. Basic income plus joint annuity	3. Basic plus 4% increasing annuity	4. Basic plus RRIF	5. Balance remaining in the fund
1	$29 587	$35 490	$31 693	$27 841	$100 590
5	$32 546	$37 461	$35 706	$31 648	$111 880
10	$35 800	$39 630	$40 381	$36 970	$121 190
15	$39 646	$42 194	$45 982	$43 139	$110 906
20	$43 788	$44 954	$51 438	$46 457	$106 280
25	$48 522	$48 109	$60 090	$51 126	$85 930

*The above information for the annuities provided by Cannex Financial Limited. The information for the RRIF provided by Polson Mac-Stephen

13
PUT YOUR AFFAIRS IN ORDER

a. LEGAL MATTERS

Everyone has had the experience of looking for something that he or she is certain is around somewhere but can't find. Years later, it turns up in some unexpected place. This may have caused expense, an opportunity lost, or other trouble. Should anything happen to you, how will others find your necessary and valuable papers? There is a simple answer: keep them all together in a secure yet easily found place, make a record of them all, and tell several people where they are kept.

Which documents are important?

(a) Your birth certificate (required for insurance and other purposes)

(b) Your social insurance number (for pensions and many financial matters)

(c) Your marriage certificate (to certify the legal position of your spouse or children)

(d) A list of any safety deposit boxes and their location, box and key numbers (they are not the same), and the location of the keys

(e) All securities you own and their location (It is generally advisable to have them registered.) Keep the purchase invoices, if they are available, and attach to the certificate to establish cost for capital gains or losses. If you do not have them, list cost prices and attach any supporting evidence such as cancelled cheques, records, and correspondence.

(f) The location and date of your current will so no one will act on an earlier, outdated one

(g) All your insurance policies and their location (fire, life, etc.)

(h) Details of property ownership, cost, mortgages, location of deed, tax bills, etc.

(i) Leases, if any

(j) Debts

(k) Any other legal paper of significance

(l) A statement of any powers of attorney you have granted

(m) Burial plans, if you have made them

1. Power of attorney

A power of attorney is valuable should you become seriously ill or incapacitated and unable to act on your own behalf. If this occurs, those caring for you either will not be able to do anything with respect to transactions, such as the sale of securities, which officially require your sanction, or will have to go through the cumbersome and expensive process of obtaining a court order to act for you. Both spouses should have one, as both signatures are required on some legal documents.

A properly executed power of attorney gives someone the power to act on your behalf in such cases. Obviously, this authority should be granted only after very careful consideration and to a person or people whom you can trust completely. The legal responsibilities and considerations attached to granting this kind of authority are fully discussed in the *Power of Attorney Kit*, another title in the Self-Counsel Series.

2. Why have a will?

Failure to leave a will when you die is a serious and costly mistake. More than half the Canadians who died last year left no will. Most people don't make a will until someone close to them dies without one. Only then, when they see the extra problems and expense caused by this omission, do they realize its importance and have one drawn up.

It is very important for both partners to have up-to-date wills. Make sure that your will reflects your current wishes about the disposal of your estate. If your disposable assets, family responsibilities (including a divorce or remarriage), or other preferences change, your will must be changed as well.

Many people dislike this task, but don't let that stop you. It is easy, takes very little time, effort, or expense and, when completed, the will can be filed away until needed or until changing circumstances require a revision. It is the *only* way you can direct the execution of your wishes and responsibilities after you have gone efficiently and by executors of your choice at a known cost.

The cost of a state-directed disposal of your property will be more expensive than the normal procedure with a will. If there is no will, a court appoints an executor to divide the assets according to provincial law. This may be very different from what you would like. A substantial part could go to children and relatives, and only the remainder to your spouse, for example. This could prevent your spouse from continuing to live at the income level expected.

3. Your will

Your will should dispose of your assets in the manner you choose and to the people you desire. It should be properly drawn to ensure its acceptability to the courts and to avoid litigation. It should also take into account how to keep various taxes at a legal minimum.

The requirements of a will are well established and you can make your own. Self-Counsel Press, the publishers of this book, have published do-your-own-will guides for Ontario, British Columbia, Alberta, Manitoba, and Saskatchewan. It is relatively easy to draw up your own will as long as you have a guide to assist you. If you have a complex situation, such as trust arrangements and a substantial estate, you should see a lawyer. Charges for estate planning and will drafting are in the range of $75 to $150 an hour, but the money is well spent for the peace of mind it gives you.

b. FUNERAL PLANS — THE UNPOPULAR TOPIC

1. Your funeral

It is wise to make decisions about your funeral long before you expect to die. Doing so won't make any difference to you, but it certainly will to your survivors because then they will be spared this problem at a difficult time. Your death will be a shock to your spouse and family, and any assistance you can render by making advance preparations will be valuable and appreciated.

There are very few of us who can face going through the complete list of steps through to arranging the details of the actual funeral. This is best done when time is available to consider the alternatives and a decision can be made on a logical, rather than emotional basis.

The following is a partial list of decisions to be made. Complete as many as you wish, but always remember to advise those who are likely to be responsible for their implementation about your decisions.

(a) If you wish, talk with a funeral director or get details from a memorial society, and have your next-of-kin with you. Most funeral directors will be happy to discuss arrangements and costs and they can also give good advice on such things as whether the service should be public or private, whether friends should be given the opportunity to visit, or whether it should be a strictly family burial with a notice after the event that it has taken place. An experienced director can tell you what others have found satisfactory, and what they have found to be serious mistakes.

(b) Acquaint your family with your wishes for the actual service, but consider the beliefs and wishes of your spouse as well. He or she will want to feel included in this last act for you. A funeral that leaves your family satisfied can be important for helping them adjust to the loss. Also remember that if you plan for something that is not to the liking of your family, the final arrangements can be changed by your next-of-kin at the time of your death.

(c) Decide if you wish cremation or burial. If you want to be cremated, how should the ashes be disposed of? If you choose burial, where will it be? Now is the time to find out if there is room in a family plot or, if you need to make arrangements, to look around, compare costs, and pay for one. Prices may vary for a plot in a churchyard, in a publicly operated non-profit cemetery, or in one operated by a private organization.

(d) The final step is making the actual arrangements with the funeral director. The best way to avoid complaints about the cost of funerals is to make suitable arrangements in advance. Some directors will accept prepayment of many expenses.

2. Memorial societies

The Memorial Society Association of Canada is a non-sectarian, non-profit organization that helps its members preplan an inexpensive, simple funeral. There are 20 member associations and two non-member societies located from coast to coast in Canada. They have done the investigating as to what is necessary and what is optional, and they provide this information together with specific recommendations to enable members to decide what they want in a funeral. There are many similar societies throughout the United States that will co-operate with a Canadian society should the death of one of its members occur there.

The biggest advantage of being a member of this society is that decisions respecting the funeral are made when time is available in non-emotional circumstances. The surviving family is spared the problem of arranging the funeral at a time when it is most difficult for them to do so.

If you are interested, you should contact the nearest association for an application form. Membership costs vary, but generally run from $5 to $10 for a lifetime membership. On joining, you will be provided with information describing the various procedures that are required and those that are optional. Package funeral costs are available from participating funeral directors. These packages provide the necessary basics, and arrangements for extras can be made. Much useful information on the comparative costs of cremation, cemetery plots, and burial procedures is included.

c. THINK OF YOUR SPOUSE!

When making your will, changing life insurance, or purchasing an annuity or pension plan, be sure to consider your spouse's position if he or she survives you. Often this is not considered and bequests are made to children or charity without realizing the hardship put on the surviving spouse. Therefore, you should take into account the expenses and the changes that will occur after you die and be certain to provide in full for your spouse first, unless you have made a decision to the contrary with full knowledge of what you are doing.

With the elimination of death duties, it may be that there will be no taxes payable. Your lawyer or accountant can advise you if anything will be payable in your case. The province you live in and the location of the assets, as well as the value of the estate, may have a bearing; each case should be considered individually.

If you wish to make bequests to others, you can do so by a trust with a life interest to your spouse as explained later. Alternatively, both partners can make their wills at the same time and word them to reflect their joint wishes so that the desired distribution will be achieved after the second has passed away, regardless of which one goes first.

In either case, if so willed, the surviving spouse has the assets or full income for life and bequests are left to others after this obligation has been fulfilled.

1. The cost of dying

The expenses at the time of death are the funeral costs and probate and executor's fees. (In many cases, survivors may be able to save on legal fees by doing the probate themselves using *Probate Guide*, another title in the Self-Counsel Series.) Funerals cost from $1 000 to

$5 000, depending on how elaborate the arrangements are. Lawyer's fees for probate average about 2% of the gross value of the estate. Finally, executors, unless they are also beneficiaries, will receive 2% to 4% of the gross value of the estate. There also may be outstanding debts, and perhaps taxes, although these are unlikely on a small estate passing to a spouse.

If the surviving spouse requires all available income, it may be unfair to divide it with others at this time. If there is no life insurance, the money for final expenses must be drawn from savings and investments that will reduce your spouse's income accordingly.

2. Changes in income on the passing of the first partner

(a) Old Age Security Pension

The Old Age Security Pension ceases with death. The surviving spouse continues to receive any pension already payable in his or her own right.

Previously, a Spouse's Allowance pension was cancelled on the death of the pensioner's spouse. This has been changed and the pension will continue until superseded by the Old Age Security Pension at age 65.

(b) Canada or Quebec Pension Plan

Providing a pensioner had contributed for one-third of the number of calendar years possible, or for 10 years, whichever is the smaller, or at least 3 years in any case, the surviving spouse of either a legal marriage or a common-law relationship may be eligible for a monthly pension as may dependent children.

If the contributor had never received a pension but was contributing to the plan, at death it is assumed that he or she had reached 65 and a pension is calculated on which to base the survivor's benefits. In either case, there is a monthly pension as shown in Sample #8. The formula differs according to whether the person receiving it has reached 65. It also depends on whether or not he or she now receives a Canada or Quebec Pension.

SAMPLE #8
MAXIMUM CANADA PENSION PLAN
SURVIVOR'S BENEFITS

	1992
Death benefit (maximum)	$3 220
Surviving spouse's maximum monthly pension	
65 or over	381.67
Under 65	352.71
(Plus survivor's own Canada Pension — total cannot exceed $636.11	

(a) If the survivor is under 65, the maximum CPP payment for 1992 was $352 per month. (It is related to the size of the spouse's pension.)

(b) If the survivor has reached 65 and does not have a Canada Pension already, he or she receives 60% of the deceased's pension to a maximum amount of $381.

(c) A surviving spouse already receiving a Canada Pension is entitled to the larger of either —

    (i) 100% of his or her own pension in addition to 37½% of the deceased's pension, or

    (ii) 60% of his or her present pension and 60% of the deceased's pension.

Total under (i) or (ii) cannot exceed the maximum starting pension ($636 in 1992).

(See Table #1 for Quebec Pension Plan benefits.)

Spouses' pensions and orphans' benefits commence the month following the month in which the contributor died subject to certain 12-month retroactive provisions. In the case of a widow who gives birth to a contributor's child following the death of the contributor, orphans' benefits commence with the month following the month of the child's birth.

When a spouse to whom a monthly survivor's benefit is payable remarries, survivor benefits after remarriage are no less than 60% of the level received by the deceased spouse.

If the second spouse dies, the survivor then becomes eligible for a pension equal to the one discontinued or the one that may be payable as a result of the death of the second spouse, whichever is greater.

Should the second marriage end in divorce or annulment, the pension previously paid as a result of the death of the first spouse may again become payable when the Canada Pension Plan administration is notified. When the surviving spouse dies, the monthly survivor's benefit ceases as of the month following the month in which the death occurred.

There is also a death benefit that is a lump sum of six times the monthly pension. But it cannot exceed 10% of the maximum pensionable earnings for that year. Those not entitled to maximum benefits may receive smaller payments.

(c) Private or industrial pension plans

Find out exactly what your survivors are entitled to if you are enrolled in a pension plan. There are many variations and it is very possible that, on the pensioner's death, there will be a basic reduction or complete cessation of the payments to the survivor.

(d) Life insurance

So far, we have considered incomes that will be reduced by death. The major common source of a new flow of income is life insurance — this was the original reason for its purchase. Earlier, the alternatives that could be selected instead of awaiting payment at death were considered. Some enabled you to retain the life insurance while using its cash surrender value to produce income and eliminate the cost of carrying it.

Your final decision on the disposition of this insurance may now be determined more clearly after you have gone through the exercise of looking into the future position of your spouse after you die. You may direct in your will what is to be done with the proceeds, or you may simply make the policy payable to the beneficiary.

This step makes the proceeds payable directly to the beneficiary and while for tax purposes it is considered part of your estate, it is no longer under the control of the executor; the beneficiary has full use of it and can spend or invest it as desired.

Some part of the proceeds of life insurance policies may be taxable either by drawing the C.S.V. or termination at death, so policy holders should take this into account. The insurance company can advise what, if any, portion of your policy will be treated this way.

(e) Passing on RRSPs

When you die, the fair market value of your RRSP will be included as part of your income in the year of death with one exception: If the RRSP is willed to a spouse, he or she can roll it into another RRSP. This may be an important consideration for the survivor.

3. Remarriage

Remarriage should be discussed long before one of the partners dies. The terms of each spouse's will may have an effect on the benefits the surviving spouse is entitled to if he or she remarries and so may affect the surviving partner's happiness seriously.

Try to think of your spouse's position, and eliminate as much emotion and jealousy as humanly possible. The survivor will be left alone at a time when your children will have their own family affairs to concern them. There are few instances where the parents live successfully with their grown children. Friends are becoming more restricted in their activities and are passing on. Single men and women are not often included in plans with couples.

Loneliness is a major problem and the support of a partner is needed more than ever. Remarriage at this stage seems to be most frequently contracted between old friends who already know each other well. Such a union brings additional financial strength because of the pooled income and brings companionship and the prospect of a few more happy years.

Frequently, widows or widowers hold back on re-marriage thinking, "I wish I knew what my late spouse would think about it." This can be settled if you and your spouse discuss the issue now.

Remember that if your will is left as a trust with income to the survivor, it frequently stipulates that income ceases on remarriage. Such a provision is often put in without proper consideration. If you and your partner worked together to build your estate, is the survivor not entitled to continuance of it if he or she remarries? Let your decision on this matter be one that is well thought out and mutually understood and accepted by both partners.

14
CHOOSING YOUR RETIREMENT HOME

a. WHAT SHOULD IT PROVIDE?

At each stage of your life, housing has a different function to perform. Its kind, size, and location are determined by the necessities of the various stages of life. If you had children, their welfare was probably the dominant factor when they were young. Schooling and safety of access to it, availability of playmates and recreation areas, and freedom from undesirable influences may have been decisive. Most of these factors have no value and are perhaps even disadvantages after retirement.

The design of your present home may not lend itself to retirement living, and it may require too much physical effort or expensive maintenance. Any extra room, which is no longer used, is expensive to carry in terms of taxes, heat, and upkeep. The money it is worth is tied up unproductively instead of producing income for you. Unless these costs can be offset by renting the extra space out, taking in boarders, or "duplexing," you have sufficient reason to think about moving.

The primary function of a house is the provision of shelter; your home is the place in which you eat, sleep, keep your clothes and slippers and which you use as a base — in short, where you "live." For many, their homes are merely night time shelters for they spend much of their day away at outside interests. To others the home provides all, or almost all, of their activities, and they spend most of their days there, going out

193

infrequently. They are home-centred and spend little time or money elsewhere. Their homes take the place of other people's clubs and outside pursuits.

The next important factor is location. It should be near the places you frequent. If it is convenient for shopping, church, the library and other places of interest, transportation will not be a problem. If it is a problem, you may not make the effort. If it is convenient for friends and relatives to come, they may drop in frequently, but if difficult, they may avoid doing so. If inconvenient, merchants may not deliver and service people might refuse to come. Obviously, location can place you in either an isolated situation and result in the loss of much that is valuable, or place you in the midst of those things that are important to you, therefore facilitating your enjoyment of them.

Retirement brings the need to replace the time spent at employment with new interests and perhaps changes to cope with a reduced income. It may be time to give up physically demanding work. Easily available health care assistance may be advisable. There may be a need to find new friends. The home you choose may well be the most important factor in making adjustments and determining the quality of life. Your present home may be quite satisfactory, but it is time to consider alternatives. There are many options specially conceived to provide all these conveniences for retired persons.

Many who have been living in a house find the advantages of an apartment or some form of retirement community desirable or necessary. Convenience, new friends, and new facilities may come with a multiple dwelling unit or retirement community, but new restrictions may also be introduced. Talk with people living in any new place which you may be considering. Most people will tell you about advantages and the problems. And then, if you decide to live there, you will already know your neighbors.

There is also the cost factor. It might be easier for you to rent or to buy something else. Consider all the factors discussed in this and the following chapter.

b. WHAT SHOULD IT COST?

A common question is "What percentage of our income should be spent on housing?" There is no figure that applies to everyone; each person's situation should be considered individually. It is a good question, but the decision should not be based on cost alone, for the home chosen may affect many aspects of life and often determines the success of adjustment to retirement.

When you consider how much you are going to spend on a new home, you need to total the house, transportation, and entertainment, for they affect each other and cannot be treated independently. This means that the money available for each of these three items should be pooled and divided to provide the most enjoyable life for you and your spouse.

Transportation can be very expensive and its cost may be an important consideration. A location that permits you to walk to most places is least expensive; public transportation is next. Lengthy automobile trips can be costly and their expense may be greater than the saving made by locating in an inexpensive but inconvenient place.

c. EVALUATING A RETIREMENT HOME

Use the following checklist to evaluate your present home for your retirement living needs and to evaluate alternatives when making a decision about whether or not to move.

(a) Does it provide the space desired?

(b) Are the facilities and fixtures suitable?

(c) Are the costs acceptable?

(d) Will it enable you to enjoy your hobbies?

(e) Is maintenance simple and not too strenuous for you?

(f) Will your furniture fit?

(g) Is it in good repair?

(h) Will redecorating be required?

(i) Is it safe or are there hazardous features?

(j) Will you be able to leave to travel?

(k) Are pets allowed, if you have one?

(l) Are shopping, health care facilities, churches, libraries, and recreational facilities available nearby?

(m) Is it accessible to both family and friends?

(n) What will transportation costs be?

(o) Is public transportation available at the required hours?

(p) Are power, water, and sewers readily available and can fire insurance and a reasonable mortgage be obtained?

(q) Will you and your spouse really enjoy living there?

(r) Will the home be suitable for the rest of your life, or will you be faced with another move?

d. MAKING THE CHOICE

The home provides different things for different people. One couple may consider it as simply a shelter that has no entertainment value and they begrudge any time spent on it. An apartment that provides the necessities, requires no attention and keeps the cost low is fine. To others, the home provides their major interests, is a source of satisfaction, and the place in which their time is happily spent. Obviously, they will be prepared to spend a larger part of their income for their home. They would be very unhappy in an apartment.

If you think that a move may be desirable, think about what you would like to have, can afford, and if you should rent or purchase. This will also narrow the choice to areas that will meet your needs and eliminate others that definitely do not.

Be prepared to spend some time in finding the home that meets your requirements. Better to spend a few months more in the search than many unhappy years later!

There is a wide range of choices, some of which you may not have considered, but which may have definite advantages and should be considered. A list of some of those which retired people have found satisfactory follows.

1. Renting

Renting does not require money for the initial purchase and it fixes basic costs. In some cases, renting will relieve you of the costs of care and maintenance. Before you rent, check the terms of the lease carefully, as you are accepting a liability that will run for some time and cannot be changed by you without the lessor's consent.

If you are not familiar with leases, it is worth having a lawyer review it.

Then look at the condition of the premises and find out who will pay for any repairs and redecorating desired. This should be understood and expressed in writing. Will all your furniture fit and be satisfactory? Changes could be costly.

Before signing the lease, talk to some of the tenants and the officers of the tenants' association if there is one. You will soon learn if there are problems with the landlord or other residents that you would want to avoid.

2. Purchasing

If your decision is to purchase, there are different considerations. (If you are purchasing a condominium, see the next section.) You will be responsible for all expenses once you own the home, so the first step is to arrange for a lawyer to go over the offer to purchase before you sign it. A lawyer's function is to see that your interests are properly protected, that all taxes and prepaid or accrued expenses are properly apportioned, and then to search the title to be sure that you get clear ownership when you pay for it.

Once the home is yours, you are fully responsible for all repairs, maintenance, upkeep, taxes, etc., so you must investigate its condition carefully before offering to buy. An offer is understood to be for purchase in its present condition unless it states that the seller agrees to do certain things, perhaps repairs or replacements.

If the seller accepts an offer, the repairs are then his or her responsibility, but you must be sure to have them written into the offer. In the case of a new, incomplete building, promises may be made that certain things will be done. Under no circumstances accept a verbal promise; have it clearly stated in the offer and retain a cash holdback (i.e., don't pay the full price, hold back a part) until these are completed. Insist on a larger holdback than the value of the work because this is often the only way to assure its prompt completion.

When purchasing a resale home, you are responsible for determining the condition of the property. There may be major expenses coming up. If you are competent to make the appraisal, do so; if not, get help. If you have a friend who understands construction and household equipment, this may do. You may prefer to hire a professional appraiser who will examine the building from basement to roof, advise if repairs and replacements are necessary now or will be in the near future, and estimate the cost.

Ask for verification of the operating costs, such as taxes and fuel, of the property. If there is a mortgage, ask to see it. Information supplied by agents may not be accurate. They list many properties and have been known to confuse the facts.

A piece of real estate is worth what someone will give for it today. Market conditions may change rapidly so the value may be different tomorrow. Realize that a real estate agent has been hired by the owner's interests, not yours. Most try to be fair, but a person can't serve two masters, so do not rely on the agent to be your adviser.

Your first move is to decide what the place is worth. You can have an appraiser help you determine the value or you can compare the property to others in the same neighborhood.

Presumably, the asking price is within your range. Homes rarely sell for exactly the asking price, some asking prices are too high, some are below the actual value. If the market is rising rapidly and demand is strong, some properties bring more than the asking price as two or more purchasers bid each other up. Others take longer to sell while the owners realize what their properties are worth and finally accept the offered price. Decide what you are willing to pay, then discuss with the seller (agent) the possibility of putting in an offer lower than the asking price. The agent is obligated to take your offer to the owner who may accept or reject it, or perhaps send it back offering a compromise.

For more information see your province's edition of the *Real Estate Buying/Selling Guide*, another title in the Self-Counsel Series.

e. CONDOMINIUMS

Condominium ownership is a legal device to make it possible to purchase, rather than rent, part of a multiple-dwelling property. The whole property is divided into self-contained living areas that are privately owned and other sections that are owned by all the owners in common. Each property must have a legal document that sets forth this division in detail, and all vary to a degree. For example, some units include the exterior building walls in the private area, others do not. This makes a difference, for if the exterior of the building is private, each owner is responsible for the maintenance of it and the window cleaning in his or her own unit; if it is owned in common, the condominium corporation will be responsible.

What you buy consists of two sections — your private apartment and the right to use all other parts of the property that are used in common by all owners. The common areas consist of everything outside the private residential units and include things such as the lobbies, passageways, service equipment, recreational facilities and so forth. A private parking space and basement storage space may or may not be included in the purchase price, or may be available at extra cost.

Usually the builder offers the units for sale as soon as the plan has been completed and construction is about to begin. The whole project remains under the builder's ownership until the required percentage of units have been sold, the building basically completed, and registration is permitted.

A condominium is a corporation with a charter which sets forth the details of division of private and common elements and similar details. It sets up by-laws under which it will be operated and how the board of directors will be elected by the unit owners and what and how changes in the by-laws can be made. Only after registration, can a full negotiable title with a deed be obtained for the unit for which you have paid. With the deed the property can be mortgaged, sold, or rented just as any other property, but such acts must conform to any restrictions imposed by the by-laws. Once registered, the condominium becomes a legal entity owned jointly by the owners of the individual dwelling units.

1. Operation and cost sharing

Owners are responsible for the operation and payment of a condominium. The charter specifies what percentage of the cost of operation is to be borne by each unit. It also defines what expenses will be pooled and paid for by the condominium, rather than by the individual. These often include your power, heat, water, care of common areas, and fire insurance for the entire building. This total cost is then divided and assessed to each owner according to the charter division, and is billed monthly. This is a legal obligation and if not paid can become a charge against your property. Each owner pays private costs such as telephone and maintenance of his or her private unit.

2. Purchasing

Many of the possible traps arising when purchasing a condominium are different from those related to purchasing a house. For example, it is possible to purchase a unit either while under construction or after completion which may or may not be registered. There is considerable difference in each of these situations; for your protection sign nothing before discussing it with your lawyer.

In the early stages of construction, purchase must be made from written and verbal information. Brochures with artists' sketches and plans with room sizes and details of construction and finishing should be available. Be sure that there is adequate power, water, and drainage for the equipment you desire. Copies of the plan, by-laws, and estimated operating cost should be available. Each province sets the basic disclosures, guarantees, and protective measures required. Finished demonstration units may be available for inspection.

Buying a condominium at this stage can be risky. You usually must put down a deposit and agree to pay the balance when your unit is ready for occupancy, which may be before registration. The builder estimates a completion date which could be delayed by strikes, financial problems, etc. Construction could cease, leaving you in a bind. So if purchasing during construction, be prepared for delays. Only purchase from a builder with good financial strength and with a reputation for finishing on time, delivering well-built units, correcting deficiencies, and accurately estimating costs.

Depending on your agreement to purchase, you may be required to pay for your unit when it is ready, even if it is not registered. If so, your monthly payments are considered as rent and you are a tenant without a deed. Your lawyer can protect against problems that could arise in such circumstances.

If you purchase after completion and registration, you can inspect the unit and common areas and get the feel of the place. You can meet and talk with your neighbors and decide if you would enjoy living with them. You will learn if they are satisfied and if they propose changes. If the building has been operating for a year or more, the accuracy of the operating expenses will be known and management quality assessed. You will get a deed and an exact date for closing your purchase.

In general, if you have been living in a house or a rented apartment there may be many differences in condominium living of which you may not be aware. These could be privacy, living under majority control, inconvenience of your own and guest parking, rules about pets, garbage disposal, security problems, and elevators. Discuss such things with those experienced in condominium living; they can give valuable information.

Legislation governing condominiums comes under the jurisdiction of the provinces and all the by-laws must conform to their statutes. Condominium tenure is known as such in all provinces except British Columbia where it is known as "strata titles" and in Quebec where it is known as "co-ownership of immovable." Other than in their terminology, the laws differ little from province to province but may be greatly different in foreign jurisdictions.

3. Owner's responsibilities and costs

(a) The owner of a unit has a vote in the formation of the by-laws and must accept any responsibility or cost which they impose.

(b) Each person has the usual cost of maintaining his or her own living unit in the manner in which he or she pleases.

(c) Payment for utilities may be partly common and partly private, depending on the by-laws.

(d) Separate real estate taxes are levied on each unit just as they would be on a house.

(e) If there is a mortgage, it is on your unit and you are responsible for payment.

(f) Insurance on the unit may be covered adequately and be paid for in the monthly fee, or you may elect to purchase additional insurance at your own expense.

(g) At the time of purchase, there are the expenses related to any real estate transactions, such as legal fees, adjustments and transfer taxes.

4. Some advantages of condominium ownership

(a) You own your own home. This means security of tenure as there is no lease to be terminated.

(b) You can usually purchase similar space at a lower price than you would pay for a free standing house.

(c) Part of your capital may be released and is available for income-producing investment or perhaps the purchase of a summer or winter holiday home.

(d) Your money is invested in your own home. It produces no taxable income in Canada. Tax impacts may be very different in a foreign country.

(e) Your capital is invested in real property that may turn out to be a hedge against inflation. Under present laws, if it is your principal residence, there will be no tax on any profit made when it is sold.

(f) Ownership will control one of the components of rent. If the value of a rental unit increases, the owner usually increases the rent. This you will avoid. Improvements you pay for increase the value of your property. When renting, they benefit the owner.

(g) Your unit can be mortgaged, but it is often more economical to buy outright if you can.

(h) You are freed of many of the responsibilities of property maintenance and operation.

(i) You participate in management and can express your wishes and cast your vote. When renting you may not be consulted when changes affecting you are being considered.

(j) The cost of major items, such as a swimming pool, is divided among all owners, which may make such facilities available that you could not afford to purchase yourself.

5. Some disadvantages of ownership

(a) You surrender some independence and become subject to majority control.

(b) Cost decisions are group decisions. As an example, you may be required to help pay for a swimming pool which you may not want or use.

(c) You have the responsibilities of ownership. If you wish to move you must arrange its sale or rental. If renting, you walk out at the end of the lease.

(d) The money invested is tied up and not available, although taking a mortgage could provide the major part if desired.

(e) There may be some restrictions on sale or leasing. This will depend on the by-laws of each unit.

6. What to watch for

When you are buying a condominium, you should watch for all the usual things that apply to the purchase of any home. But there are special problems that apply only to condominiums.

First, if the development has not been completed and properly registered as a condominium and turned over by the developer to the owners, you will not be able to get a deed to your property. You are simply renting from the developer. Any payments on the unit may be considered as rent until the turnover has taken place. You may have serious problems if the development takes a long time to complete or goes bankrupt.

Second, when you are purchasing at this stage, the statements of expected monthly operating costs are just estimates. They may be very misleading, so you should compare these estimates with actual costs for similar properties.

Third, the by-laws set up for the development period will all be subject to review and possible change when the owners take over. Try to meet some of the present occupants and ask if they are happy or would like to see changes.

f. CO-OPERATIVE APARTMENTS

A co-operative apartment is different from a condominium in that the co-operative owns all the property and you buy shares from it and rent your unit from it. You become responsible for the expense of the co-operative through the obligation attached to the ownership of these shares. You remain responsible until your shares have been sold and transferred to another owner.

Any mortgage, for example, is on the whole property and you have no choice but to bear your share. You may become responsible for bearing a large part of the cost of carrying vacant space, should vacancies occur. In a condominium, these costs would accrue against the owner of the vacant units and would be recovered on sale, provided the price is high enough to yield an adequate surplus.

If you contemplate purchasing shares in a co-operative apartment, be sure to understand all the obligations and implications before signing anything.

g. RENTAL APARTMENTS

The alternatives can be narrowed down if your financial situation favors rented rather than owned premises. Renting frees your capital for income production. The rental charged for such a suite may be lower than the cost of carrying the comparable living space in a house, particularly if the house is mortgaged.

For the retired person, there are a great many advantages to the rented apartment. Some rental buildings cater to young families, and some to older people without families. This can be important. (One person who lives in an apartment building occupied by her contemporaries reports that she can enjoy a card game every night with neighbors, without ever leaving the building!)

There is no physical effort required in caring for the lawn or building, or removing snow. The cost is known, which is important to anyone on a tight budget, and if you wish to be free to travel or go off to the cottage, things will be looked after during your absence.

h. MOBILE OR MANUFACTURED HOMES

1. What are they like?

Just what is a mobile home? If you have not been in a modern mobile home (now often called a manufactured home), you may be very agreeably surprised when you see one.

The increase in the sale of mobile homes for use as permanent dwellings has been rapid. If you visit dealerships where mobile homes are sold, it will soon become apparent that retired couples are buying many of them.

There are two types of mobile units which are frequently confused. The trailer or RV provides temporary, compact accommodation that can be taken along as you travel. The "mobile home" has a similar exterior appearance to a trailer but is much larger. In spite of the name, it is no longer really mobile in the same sense as the trailer. It is usually much too large to be towed by an ordinary automobile and is not equipped with its own wheels. It is taken on a large truck to a location where it is set up on a permanent foundation. (It is now common to build a basement and place this "mobile" on top.) In reality, mobile homes are factory-built homes, designed so they can be transported as units then set up on permanent foundations and left there the same as any other house.

Regular "parks" provide sewers, water, and electricity which are permanently connected. The unit is mobile when compared with a standard house only in that it can be picked up from the foundation and moved to a new location if and when desired.

Mobile homes are meant to be permanent dwellings. They are well-designed and durable and many are built by established, reputable companies. They come in either single or double widths. The singles are about three to five metres wide and frequently as long as twenty metres. The doubles are built in two sections, divided down the middle so that the two halves, when assembled side by side, make up dwellings that are approximately twice as wide as the single units. They must be built in this manner so that they can be transported by road in the usual way and joined together on the site. They provide homes of more common proportions up to nine metres in width, which permits wider rooms and a centre hall. They are often spacious and may have a living room, a dining room, den, one to three bedrooms, kitchen, utility room, and bathroom.

If they are placed on a regular basement, a workshop and storage space can help keep the floor warmer in winter. A canopy to cover a patio is common.

Appliances are usually modern and smart. The bathroom may have modern fixtures, a built-in vanity and counter-top, and mirrors and exhaust fans. Size and space is little problem unless you are looking for unusually large rooms. Equipment may include a freezer, refrigerator, electric or propane stove, double stainless steel sink, and built-in cupboards and counters. Each model is usually offered in an assortment of interior decorator designed color schemes. Some even have woodburning fireplaces.

When you purchase a standard house, the lot is part of the package. But, in the case of mobiles, the location on which to place it is usually a separate deal (although some parks do provide the site and home together). You should not purchase the home until you have selected and obtained the site, possibly the most difficult part. You are not free to park the unit on any available land that can be purchased or rented because there are often land use restrictions.

Most regulatory by-laws are made by, and are under the control of, the province and the local municipality. There is little uniformity. In some rural areas, there are practically no restrictions; in others, they are treated the same as conventional structures and must conform to the land-use by-laws. In other places, municipalities have permitted separate sites to be set aside and used for mobile homes with specific provisions for them. Some are on the outskirts of towns and use all their amenities. Others are set up as independent communities with facilities of their own.

Some parks cater to all comers, but others restrict themselves to retired people. In these parks, the lots are rented by the month and the rent usually includes water and sewage services. From there on, there is no iron-clad policy. Rents vary with the location and the quality and quantity of services offered.

Obviously, the cost of renting a lot in an undeveloped rural setting is going to be small, and it is possible that an inexpensive water supply and satisfactory sanitary facilities can be installed privately. At the other end of the scale is the lot which is on high-priced land skirting a metropolis and on which paved roads, a sewage system, water, and electricity have been installed.

It is possible to sell a well-located, unmortgaged regular house for enough to buy a good mobile home and still have enough money left over for investment that could provide the income to pay the land rent and operating costs. This means that the move would save the operating costs of your present home and the extra money would then be available for other purposes.

The advantages of mobile home life are that the home is readily available at a firm price, in a finished form, often for immediate delivery. The most suitable home and lot can be selected separately and combined. The home can be purchased, and often financed, if you wish, and the lot can be rented, a choice not usually available in a regular house. The cost of the mobile is usually less than a house. It is frequently possible to select a location in which mainly retired people live if you so desire, and the home can be moved to another location at will.

2. What to watch for

When buying a mobile home, remember that all are not of the same quality and some will give less trouble and be better than others. Appraise the quality of materials and workmanship of the various makes. Only consider purchasing from an established reputable dealer, for he or she is less likely to handle an inferior product. The dealer's experience can also be valuable in assisting you with the selection of the most suitable model and options for you.

Some mobile homes are fire hazards, containing too many flammable materials, or are poorly designed so that a fire once started is difficult to contain. Another complaint is unsafe design; there are insufficient escape points and occupants could be trapped. These factors have resulted in high insurance rates and in some cases insurance cannot be purchased at all. Before buying the home or contracting for the lot, contact your insurance agent to be sure insurance is available and what it will cost.

Recently, safety standards have been upgraded, and approximately 95% to 98% of the mobile homes manufactured in Canada now meet Canadian Standards Association approval and bear its seal. This association has set standards for strength, fire resistance, weather and condensation resistance, heating, plumbing and electrical systems, design, quality of materials and safety features while in transit, according to the Canadian Mobile Home Association. The United States has excellent regulations but these are apparently not enforced in all states. Look for the seal of approval on any imported or Canadian models.

Older mobile homes may have been manufactured to lower standards, but most municipalities require that mobile homes have the approval of the local hydro-electric commission before being hooked up.

The dealer is responsible for arranging delivery and is the first contact for the correction of any repairs or deficiencies under the warranty; if the dealer is co-operative, the inevitable problems will be readily corrected without unpleasantness. Be wary of any dealer who tries to insist that any financing be done through him or her. Examine the warranty carefully and compare those offered by various makers.

Regular mortgages are available when the home is located in some well-run parks, otherwise financing is usually done on the same basis as automobiles, which means a high rate of interest. Use your own cash or borrow on other security through a bank or trust company, if necessary. Now some units, provided they are located in approved sites, are CMHC (Central Mortgage and Housing Corporation) approved, and regular

long-term mortgages are available from the usual lend-
ers.

Obtaining a suitable location on which to place the
home may be difficult. Some parks may insist that you
buy the home through them. If your intended location
is not in an established park, be sure that the local
by-laws will permit its use for your plan. One of the
great drawbacks is the shortage of suitable lots, and one
you will enjoy may be difficult to find. Obtain copies of
all rules and regulations to which any site is subject.

There are two wise steps to take before deciding on
a home or a location. First, talk to the owners of homes
of the make you are selecting, persons who have bought
from the dealer you have in mind, and those living in
the park you are considering. Visit them and see if it
seems to be a home you will enjoy. People are usually
willing and eager to either recommend or condemn,
depending on their experience, and this kind of information may save you much trouble.

Second, before purchasing the home or signing up
for a location, see your lawyer and ask him or her to
review the contract and warranty for the home and the
terms involved in renting the lot. There may be many
things you do not understand or may not have asked,
and an experienced lawyer will spot them quickly.

i. THE FINAL MOVE — A RESIDENCE
WITH MEDICAL AND NURSING
SERVICES AVAILABLE

If you are one of those who lives on to a ripe old age,
the time may come when you cannot continue to live
independently even if your spouse or a friend of similar
age lives with you. Unless you are fortunate enough to
have a younger relative or paid companion to assist,

you may find it necessary to enter a home where you will receive the required care.

Nothing generates as many heated and obstinate statements from retired people as the mention of going into a "nursing home." It is unfortunate that this is so and, as a starting point, realize that the first thing wrong is the inaccurate use of the term "nursing home." This designation is erroneously used to describe everything from a luxurious private apartment hotel building in which medical and nursing care and food services are available if desired, to a home where persons completely incapable of looking after even minor functions for themselves are fully cared for. To some, it also includes the old-fashioned "poor house" of Charles Dickens' days.

Most discussions on this topic are, therefore, conducted in a heavy fog of ignorance and misunderstanding. They always seem to carry a derogatory connotation and imply the idea of charity. Perhaps the loss of personal freedom is feared. This attitude prevents proper consideration and those who are considering them should not be discouraged. The growth of these homes has been rapid both in number and, through knowledge and experience of the requirements of their customers, in quality.

One of the most useful things that could be done in this area would be to clarify and properly classify and name each type so that those interested could identify the kind under discussion. This would separate the groups, which is desirable as there is little similarity between them.

Specialists in the field do agree that it is best for older people to operate on their own if possible. There is no move afoot to round up all older persons and to segregate them in some sort of an institution. It is recognized that they will retain their abilities longer if they use them on their own behalf, and any special provisions should be made only for those who require it. Support services may provide all that is needed.

Often individuals have moved into nursing homes because they required certain care that had to be provided by trained professionals, and these were the only places where such care was available. Now many municipalities provide and pay for the health support service such as a visiting nurse, therapist, homemaker, or others, if by so doing the person can remain independent. Ask about these services through your doctor or the local public health nurse who will know what services are available and how they can be provided.

About 7% of the population of Canada over 65 now lives in such homes, and this is higher than in most industrial countries. It is thought that with greater use of the above services this figure could be reduced to everyone's advantage.

As mentioned, there is a broad range of facilities available in retirement homes. A common type is one step removed from regular apartments. Tenants often have one large room per person or couple with a private bathroom, cupboard space, etc. They may use some of their own furniture, pictures and ornaments, which enables them to bring a few of the familiar mementos of their lives with them. There may be a common room with television and a dining room where meals are served. Breakfast may be delivered to each room. Nursing and medical services may be available and are often included in the price. This may be an important comfort. Anyone can come and go without any constraint just as you would in a regular apartment.

As loneliness is one of the difficult problems of older persons, these homes provide an answer because you live with a group that can provide instant companionship. What better place to find, perhaps, a real friend? There are usually activities such as bingo, cards, and dances available. Such residences have been happy homes for many who have no handicap and don't need the extra facilities but enjoy living in this atmosphere. Others with some physical or medical disability find the provision for health care a very helpful form of security.

Retirement homes are not the answer for everyone. Someone who must have a garden, a basement workshop, and who makes his or her own opportunities may find that these are essential for happiness. The "loner," who just can't stand crowds and does not enjoy group activities does not fit in. Too often those responsible for the welfare of older relatives know of one person who is happy in such a residence and, without stopping to compare the two persons, accepts this as the answer for the second. It may not be so, for the relative may have a personality unsuited for this life.

Beyond the apartment described above, alternatives range from places where only slightly more care is given, up to those where patients receive what is equivalent to full invalid's bed care.

If you have some disability, a move to a retirement home may be very desirable and comforting. If you have a health problem, there may be very little alternative. Proper care may be essential. This is a matter to discuss and decide with your physician.

An older person, living alone, particularly if he or she has mobility or health problems, may lose interest in food, find difficulty in participating in activities with others, and become a recluse. This may contribute to mental and physical deterioration. Such an individual may benefit greatly from proper diet and health care. It may lead to a better attitude and improvement of retention of mental faculties because of the participation in a more normal and interesting social life.

If you are making a choice for yourself, or are finding a home for a relative, by all means investigate any place you are considering. Go personally, talk to the residents, go through the building, try and see the meals being served. Be critical and careful.

The most important feature of any retirement home may be the attitude of the staff to the residents. Many who work in the field think that mental activity is retained and the symptoms of aging delayed if the residents are treated with respect as responsible adults and encouraged to make decisions rather than ordered around like children. A person treated as incapable comes to accept the fact that this is so, and many who are considered senile are not.

Some places have single rooms, others offer only multiple occupancy. A convenient location that your friends and relatives can easily visit, and from which transportation is available to shopping and other places of interest is an advantage. A choice of suitable activities will make for pleasant days, and it is in this area that great strides are being made. It is increasingly recognized that providing proper food, shelter, and medical care is not enough. Participation with others is not only a source of happiness but also contributes greatly to the maintenance of health. The better homes now have extensive internal programs and also arrange group trips out to shop, visit the country, or do other interesting things. This helps you retain the feeling of being a part of the world rather than being shut off from it.

j. CARING FOR AN ELDERLY RELATIVE OR SPOUSE

During your retirement, you may be responsible for a parent or spouse who reaches the stage where he or she cannot continue to live independently. There is danger of accident, deteriorating health from lack of care, and malnutrition from improper eating habits. A person in this state may turn inward as it becomes more difficult to go out and participate. These factors together with loneliness and fear lead to unhappiness which may further accelerate the decline.

The elderly often persist in continuing in this sorry state rather than risking the unknowns of change. But although a change may not be ideal it would surely be an improvement. What should be done? It is difficult to force the move against a loved one's wishes, but it may be the greatest kindness.

If the move can be made into some family setting acceptable to all concerned, that is the best solution. People at this stage become almost childlike in their dependence on others and it is a comfort to be with relatives. Life has little to offer, there is no future, and the family to which they devoted much of their lives and which they helped to create is the one remaining thing which they hold dear. However, this option is not always possible either for lack of space or because such a move might place too great a strain on the household. This is particularly true if the older person requires care, or has become cranky and demanding.

If you decide that your relative must enter a home the first step is for you to investigate those available locally. Some are privately operated and are more expensive for those who can afford them. (The cost covers food, shelter, and care; clothing and personal spending are extra. A range of costs may be found in your area.) Public or church-supported ones may be free or cost-shared depending on the person's financial position.

Once you have made the decision, attempt to obtain agreement on the advantages of making the move, for experience shows that the person who makes it willingly adjusts more easily to the change. It is a big dislocation to close up one's home and move into a new environment with strangers, but there are many advantages. The care that will become increasingly important is available, and the lonely life, often restricted to a room or two, is replaced with companionship and activities. These may be important factors in maintaining interest in life and mental alertness.

If you decide to move your relative into such a residence, you will probably worry about his or her happiness, and, truthfully, your relative may *not* be happy. You must expect this reaction and be prepared to cope with it. The comparison is relative, however, for he or she may not only be happier but safer and more comfortable than if left in the previous difficult circumstances. The change is great, and comes at an age where it is difficult to adjust and the first period of weeks or months may be ones of constant complaints and pleas to "get me out of here."

The greatest fear of the elderly is to be placed in a home and forgotten; the greatest joy is an invitation to visit the family and see the grandchildren; phone calls, letters, and visits are bright spots in their lives.

For more information on caring for an elderly relative, see *Taking Care*, another title in the Self-Counsel Series.

15
WHERE WILL YOU LIVE?

Perhaps you have always dreamed of moving on retirement to another country to experience different and more interesting activities or a better climate. Maybe you want to give up city life and buy that acreage in the country you've always admired. There are many who do just that and write back to the folks at home describing the wonderful time they are having. But not all are so fortunate. Many return home disillusioned. Use caution, and be sure that this is the right step for you. If you have done the homework and your spouse agrees, go to it, and good luck!

a. DIFFERENT VIEWS OF MOVING

Often, spouses have very different views about moving to another country at retirement. If one of you has been working and the other staying at home for a number of years, the changes inherent in retirement are very different for each. The person retiring now has his or her whole day to replan and loses many things of value, such as the companionship of a work group. It can be very helpful to look forward to a move to some favored spot as one of the main benefits of retirement. The old associations of the job with the home can be left behind and it will be easier to get into the new routine. A completely new list of interests will be introduced.

On the other hand, a spouse who has stayed at home over the years may not want to leave the household routine and activities that are neighborhood-oriented;

moving may mean complete loss. Moving away may be a greater adjustment for a homemaker who has made the home reflect a personal lifestyle.

For these reasons, considerable compromise between the spouses may be necessary. As you consider each factor, think of the points in favor of moving and those against it. There may be a long list on both sides, but, after all are weighed, some will become unimportant. Others will gain dominance and one may soon emerge as the deciding factor that cannot be ignored. This will make your decision a definite one. You may conclude that there is no other choice.

b. FINANCIAL CONSIDERATIONS

If you have completed your estimates of retirement income and expenses and you find no financial problems, money will have no bearing on your decision to move. However, if there is going to be insufficient income to fulfil all desires, you should now be certain that you know where the shortage exists.

If the finances are going to be strained, you may help the situation by making a move, if you live in a large city, to a small town or less-expensive spot in the country. This can be a trying decision but some feel that, if they must "come down" in living style, it would be preferable not to do so in their current neighborhood. Often a move to a rural area brings savings of a major nature in addition to those from housing. For example, if you have been a member of a recreation club in any major centre, the cost has undoubtedly been high. This expense would certainly be a consideration if you are under pressure to cut your spending. In a rural area, you can usually join golf, curling, and any other clubs and participate in all the activities for a small fraction of their cost in the city. Clubs in a rural setting may not have as elaborate facilities as those in the city, but these may not be important to you. The difference in cost, on the other hand, may mean simply that you will be able to continue with the activity rather than being forced to discontinue it.

The adjustment to living on a lower income in a smaller centre is less than moving, for example, to another country, and changes do not involve the same reaction from others as in the more rigid social strata of a larger centre.

Also, it is possible to move to or near a small city or a town where excellent facilities and economical living are available, and where the location will make outdoor activities available close to home. Thus, one place doubles as a home and a cottage. There are many such communities in Canada, for example, Fredericton, Lindsay, Kelowna, Nanaimo, just to name a few across the country.

c. POSSIBILITY OF EMPLOYMENT

One of the important considerations in location is the possibility of employment, either full- or part-time. Post-retirement jobs are scarce, so if you want to have a suitable one, this will probably decide the location in which you will live.

If this consideration is important to you, be certain of the job possibilities available in any place you plan to locate. In many "retirement communities," there are many job seekers and very few opportunities. Some areas also refuse to grant work permits to individuals until they have resided there for a reasonably lengthy qualifying period. Check out all these things first to avoid serious disappointment.

d. SHOULD YOU STAY NEAR YOUR OLD JOB?

Unless your previous employer is providing work for you after you have retired, you will likely find, as many others have, that the place where you worked has very little further interest in you. Your old friends there are now as fully occupied as you were. If you visit the plant or office, they are too busy to spend much time with you. It will be unusual if they need your advice and certainly the person who took your job won't want to admit that it can't be done without your help.

All this means that it won't provide much of an interest and to be near to it and not wanted by it may be disappointing. Thus, remaining is unlikely to be of value and may be a disadvantage.

e. MILDER CANADIAN AREAS

Climate may not be the most important factor; to many the pull back home to where there are still relatives, activities, and a lifestyle they grew to enjoy when younger, may have the stronger appeal. But for those wanting a change from long cold winters, there are two Canadian areas to consider. South Vancouver Island and the Vancouver area are the better known. These areas have a sea-moderated climate, a short winter with little snow, and little hot weather in summer. There is more rain and humidity than in many other areas, but, on the whole, the longer mild season is enjoyed by many retired people.

The other area is the southern inland section of British Columbia in the Okanagan Valley and adjacent districts. The winters are short with some cold weather; the summers warm and dry. There are beautiful lakes, low mountains, and much beauty. Land and house costs are reasonable, the area is uncrowded, and the way of life is leisurely. No wonder it is becoming a popular retirement centre, particularly for those who require a dry climate.

f. MOVE TO A FOREIGN COUNTRY WITH CAUTION!

One of the possibilities that couples consider is moving to the warmer climate of a foreign country. If you make a full change of residence, you may not be required to give up Canadian citizenship, but for tax and legal purposes you will probably be under the jurisdiction of your adopted country. If you retain Canadian residence and spend a part of each year here, you can probably keep your present Canadian status and will be treated as a visitor when abroad.

The treatment for pension and health care services may be totally different in each of these cases so, before making either move, determine the effects on your status.

1. What can you gain or lose?

The obvious advantage to moving to a foreign country is usually a warmer climate, but there can be a hot or humid season that may be unpleasant. If the year-round conditions are suitable, you can enjoy a more active and enjoyable outdoor life and the selection of a suitable climate may alleviate arthritic or bronchial conditions.

Taxes and living costs may be lower in many countries. Some people hope for more economical living in a low-cost area. On the other hand, there is the problem of health care, which becomes more important with each passing year. Are you prepared to give up your provincial health insurance? Will you accept the medical facilities, and when old age and perhaps separation from your spouse comes, will satisfactory living arrangements be available? Further, are you prepared to live under the laws of your adopted country?

2. Possible language difficulties

If you are thinking of moving to a country that uses a language you do not speak, consider the special difficulties. If you don't learn the new language, you can often be in a difficult position, often seriously so, if ill or in trouble.

In many places, English or French is spoken but this may be confined to certain shops or to a colony of visitors. Unless you are willing and able to learn the new language, the inability to communicate elsewhere may become irritating and this is frequently why persons who emigrate to, for example, Greece or Mexico, eventually return home.

3. The best of both worlds

Often, retired people decide to move permanently to another country because it is less expensive than maintaining two homes. But if you can afford to have both, the best part of each year can be spent in each. As well, you can maintain closer ties with family and friends and keep that valuable medical/hospital retirement home connection which may soon become important to you and your spouse.

4. Some tax, pension, and benefit considerations

If you establish residence elsewhere, you may lose some of the government-sponsored financial benefits. Before you decide to move, you should know what this will mean to you and keep in mind that it may create tax complications.

(a) Old Age Security Pension and Canada Pension Plans

You will continue to receive your Old Age Security Pension wherever you reside provided you have resided in Canada for a total of 20 years after reaching the age of 18. If you do not fulfil the residency requirements, it is payable for only six months abroad. (The Spouse's Allowance terminates after a six-month absence; however, both spouses can continue to draw the Old Age Security if eligible.)

Canada Pension is payable to the pensioner regardless of location of residence.

(b) Capital gains tax

On moving to a foreign country, whether you sell your assets in Canada or not, a "deemed" liquidation may have occurred in the eyes of the tax department, and any theoretical capital gain that would result becomes taxable. Thus, part of your income-earning base may be lost if you emigrate. Find out by consulting an expert.

(c) Income tax

If the assets from which your income will be derived remain in Canada, you should check what the tax liabilities will be, since many types of income from Canadian sources are subject to withholding tax. Moreover, these may vary with the country to which you emigrate and you could be assessed tax in both countries.

(d) Health insurance

Government-supported health plans generally terminate when the insured moves out of the country. Some countries have plans of their own that may satisfy you. Others may not. Investigate this feature at any place in which you plan to take up residence.

Those who have disabilities requiring costly drugs or treatment, or illnesses of which they can reasonably expect a recurrence, find the protection provided by the provincial medical and hospital insurance is an asset they cannot afford to give up, unless a similar one is available where they propose to reside. For example, a friend in the United States pays $3 200 per annum for insurance that is not as inclusive as Canadian provincial plans, nor does it provide the same long-term coverage.

Private plans available at the proposed new location may have unacceptable exceptions or may be too costly. This consideration is frequently the reason for deciding against moving.

Your provincial health plan may extend coverage that protects you when on a holiday outside your borders. If you plan to spend some months outside Canada, investigate the coverage provided you during that period by your provincial health plan.

Medical and hospital costs in the United States and many other countries are frequently much greater than in Canada, and the provincial plans will only pay their provincial rate for out-of-country treatment. You could be left with a crippling balance to pay if seriously ill. This extra expense can be covered by purchasing out-of-country health insurance before leaving Canada.

g. HEALTH

The maintenance of good health now is an important consideration. Moving to a new home, for all or part of the year, may be advised by your doctor. However, if you are not content in a new environment, you might do as much harm as good, so exercise considerable care in selecting a new spot.

It is not unusual to meet people who moved to a more suitable climate only to find that the other disadvantages were too great and that they were not able to accept them or enjoy the new location. Soon they were back home again, sadder and poorer for the experience.

h. PROXIMITY TO FAMILY AND FRIENDS

Family and old friends usually mean much to retired people, and one of the common reasons for coming back given by those who moved away is that they just missed them too much and nothing else took their place.

Families cannot be replaced by new ones in another location and good friendships take years to develop. Those who move into new locations report that while newcomers are welcomed and included, no depth or real friendship seems to grow. One person moves out, another in, and no one seems to care.

i. THE RETIREMENT COMMUNITY

One recent development is the "retirement community." Many of the early ones were not conceived as such, but just developed because they filled a gap. Retired people, when they found suitable spots, began to congregate with their trailers and mobile homes. This demonstrated there was a need for properly planned communities, and some large, prosperous companies have grasped the opportunity to build towns that are specifically designed and located for retired people.

Retirement communities have been designed to take care of the specific needs of the older person. The apartments are equipped with specialized conveniences such as non-slippery floors and grab bars at the toilet and bath. Maintenance problems can be kept to a minimum and children's considerations have been eliminated.

Schools are not required and recreation and medical facilities suitable for older people are emphasized. While these physical arrangements are desirable, the main advantage may be the availability of a large number of potential companions who share similar interests. Through them, loneliness can be avoided and the provision of a broad choice of activities specially suitable for the group is made possible.

For the gregarious person who has decided to move anyway and who seeks and needs this type of life, it has decided advantages. On the other hand, those who wish to live a quieter life and whose interests do not require the participation of others may find the community too busy and privacy often difficult to maintain.

Once again, it's up to you to make the choice and fulfil your desires. These communities are available now both in Canada and abroad and are increasing in number. Many offer anyone interested a week's stay free or at low cost to try it out.

j. TRY IT OUT FIRST!

Don't make the mistake of moving to some distant point with which you are not really familiar or that you know only by the descriptions of friends or by a short holiday in the region. Living permanently somewhere is much different than vacationing there. If you move there, you will be staying in a different place, doing different things, and the glamour that comes with a holiday soon wears off.

What will it be like when you must spend year after year there? Look at all aspects carefully. Can you afford it? Are there activities you require, not only to use your time pleasantly but to provide those psychological satisfactions you require? Are there hospitals and medical facilities? What about that health insurance problem?

Can you obtain the insurance you require? Is the climate, on a year-round basis, acceptable? If you have friends and family that mean much to you, will you be able to see them often enough?

There is only one way to answer these questions to your satisfaction, and that is to have a try-out before making a permanent move. You should actually live there for as long as possible before making the step a definite one. Rent the kind of living accommodation you plan to use. Move in as a permanent resident, not a tourist, and live as you plan to live. Try out the activities in which you plan to participate. Meet the people you will have to live with once you are there.

Will you enjoy living with them? Stay on through the most unpleasant period of the year. Stay long enough for the novelty to wear off and the problems to develop. Rent out your present home for perhaps six months or a year. Any difference in cost will be well worth it, and will be much less than the cost of selling, relocating, and then doing it all over again if the move turns out to be undesirable.

16
YOUR HEALTH AND RETIREMENT
by Paul D. Clarke, M.D.

For most of us, the magic number "65" has been held up as the finishing line. Compulsory Retirement, Pension Plan, RRSP, Old Age Benefits, "Goodbye and Good Luck!"

Happily, society is re-examining this arbitrary cut-off age. Why someone doing a good job at age 64.9 years is thought to be incapable a few weeks later is beyond me. Winston Churchill started in office in May, 1940, a few weeks after his 65th birthday. I know a medical person who was "retired" by the University Teaching Hospital; he spent the next three years in Africa teaching, practising, and running a new medical school. Anyone at 65 who is healthy and active should have the right to work.

The pessimists say that in this inflationary age with the eroding value of pension plans, we will all have to stay in harness forever.

Despite these diverse factors, 65 is still retirement age for the next few years. It is important to realize that despite all the changes that will occur on that day, your mind and body don't change into a retirement phase.

The progression from late middle age (55 to 65) to the "young old" age group (65 to 75) is slow and continuous. Nothing sudden and dramatic will happen, as it does from age 10 to 15. The important thing is to *preserve what you have*. The ancient Greeks taught us "that which is not used, atrophies." An active body will be firmly muscled. Two years of inactivity will cause great muscle shrinking. The same process will happen to your mind if you don't keep it "in gear" and busy.

a. FIND SOMETHING TO DO

A soldier-poet in the trenches in 1917 wrote that if he lived through Flanders, he would "sit on my ass for 50 years, then hang my hat on a pension." Anything was an improvement over the Western Front, no doubt! This "do nothing" policy is unwise for the rest of us. You should plan what you are going to *do* with yourself when you reach retirement age.

Just as you plan your financial future, you must plan for your activities. Many of you have hobbies and interests that you are looking forward to fully developing. Many will carry on working. Those who don't want to work after 65 and have not developed any leisure time pursuits are at risk.

The sudden break from a lifetime of struggle will be wonderful...for a few weeks. Then what? There are just not that many odd jobs around the house and garden to keep you "tuned up." Daytime TV is an easy way to pass the time. You can always look out the window...or listen to the radio. Two or three years of this type of voluntary inertia (a polite way of saying "hog lazy") will produce a bored and very dull person. The odds are great that depression will set in. Then you can sit and worry all day about that sore back or that headache you had last week.

A vicious circle of pain-worry-depression leading to more pain-worry-depression can be set up. Any pain or discomfort is influenced by the state of mind. This is all too common after retirement. Many times the basic cause of vague pains is not diagnosed immediately by

232

the doctor. This leads to tests and more visits to the doctor's office. This, of course, causes more stress, more worry, and the vicious circle rolls on.

This is the background to a situation we have all heard of on occasion — death within a year or two of retirement. "Never sick a day in his life, just up and died last week."

Convinced? Please, keep busy!

b. MAINTAINING GOOD HEALTH

Having decided not to "go to seed" upon starting retirement is a major first step. The next step is to consider the rule of sensible living that our mothers taught us years ago. Today, this is called lifestyle counselling. The TV ads and the papers and magazines are full of all sorts of advice these days. You can't follow all these multimedia instructions, but you should consider making changes in your various activities and habits.

1. Exercise

A degree of physical fitness is a good thing because you feel better. Stress problems are fewer because we cope better with stress if the body is in shape. You don't have to go into Olympic training, but daily exercise is advised. The cheapest, easiest, and most readily available is a brisk 15-minute walk.

It may take a while to build up to being able to do 15 minutes of non-stop walking, but there's no hurry. The heart and lungs get a good work-out and they are the most important. Swimming is great too, if you have access to a pool.

More vigorous exercise is fine for those who have been doing it all along. If you feel the need to jog or play tennis, see your doctor first for advice about your own unique physical capabilities.

2. Diet

Volumes are written these days about nutrition and weight loss. Many controversies exist about health foods and vitamins. "Dr. Wonderful's" latest diet to cure heart disease will be seen in all the papers next week. Much that is written is sensible. Much more is absolute bunkum.

We are in an era of concern and awareness about good nutrition. We worry about toxic fertilizers, toxic sprays on crops, and cattle dosed with medications to increase their muscle bulk. We are told to take vitamins A to Z. Lose 25 pounds or else. Drink milk, but stay away from dairy products.

For anyone who is not on a specific, prescribed diet, and just wants sensible up-to-date advice on what and how much to eat, there is one common sense rule. Whatever you do, do it slowly and sensibly and in moderation.

3. Alcohol

Our society generally accepts "social" drinking. The problem is, what is "social" drinking? If I drink only when in company, can I drink as much and as often as I want?

Doctors don't have a good definition of alcoholism. I know some teetotal M.D.s who will write "chronic alcoholism" on a patient's chart. The patient enjoys a drink or two after work and may get a bit tight at a party once a month! Other doctors define an alcoholic as "someone who drinks more than I do."

Once again, moderation is the key. Also, never use alcohol as a medicine. Don't drink to get to sleep, or to "feel better," or to "brace up" for a business or social event. Herein begins the road to alcoholism and all the dreary misery that accompanies this diagnosis.

Alcohol is socially acceptable to most of us when used to relax in good company. We all know when to say enough. Specific illnesses will preclude any alcohol, of course. Most common is an active ulcer.

Remember, medicines and alcohol do not mix! Too many deaths occur because people mix tranquilizers or pain killers with alcohol. Maybe the doctor forgot to warn them. Maybe they forgot. Maybe they thought the doctor was being a fuss-pot.

Those who take pills and alcohol together stand a very good chance of (as the Irishman said) "waking up dead in the morning."

4. Smoking

Don't smoke! It can cause lung disease; chronic bronchitis — coughing; emphysema — bad shortness of breath; lung cancer — death. It can also increase your chances of artery disease (i.e., strokes, heart attacks). These are hard, cold facts. Your mother warned you. King James I banned tobacco smoking in his court.

However, many people enjoy smoking and do not want to quit. We do not live in a rational world, and wanting to smoke is a purely emotional decision. If you are in this group, I would ask you to cut down. Some doctors are pretty tough with smokers and will discharge them from the practice if they won't quit. Personally, I think this is abandoning a patient, which I never do. (You may be a damn fool, but I'll look after you.)

If you smoke 30 cigarettes a day, ease down to 15. At least you are smoking less. You might cut down on the horrendous odds facing you. You might even convince yourself to quit altogether.

AND NOW FOLKS, FOR SOMETHING THAT OUR PARENTS PROBABLY DIDN'T TELL US ABOUT

5. Sex

Volumes are written about sex these days. Most of them seem based on techniques and ratings and read like the statistics of a world series game. The present generation really didn't invent love-making, but they are certainly much more open about it.

I think the majority of people looking at retirement planning are of an age who feel that their sex life is a private matter. In fact it is so private that they won't discuss it with their doctor. Even if they have, there is a good chance that the doctor was too ill-informed or embarrassed or shocked to offer any advice beyond "learn to live with the problem."

Sex is a pretty basic urge. It compares with hunger and thirst as far as the urge itself is concerned. Society teaches restraint from an early age, and many are reticent about discussing any sexual problem. Until recently, medical schools didn't teach doctors anything about sex therapy.

An unresolved sexual problem is a source of stress. If we can't cope with a stress we get a symptom. This might be nervousness and irritability. If we "bury" the problem, then a psychosomatic symptom will probably develop — headache, sleeplessness, ulcer, or whatever. If we don't talk about the cause, then we only get treated for the symptom. If you have a problem, tell your doctor. If the response is inadequate, ask for a referral to someone skilled in this field.

Most sexual problems are emotional in origin. In other words, they are "people" problems. If a marriage is sick, the sexual aspect of the marriage likely won't be very good either. Sex and love go together with most people. Some problems have no solution. Partners in a marriage doomed to failure likely have sexual problems that won't be resolved. If the marriage is basically sound, then problems are probably able to be helped.

Much impotence (failure to get or keep an erection) in the male is due to tension or fatigue. Sometimes it just happens. When it is an occasional event, don't worry. If it happens a lot, see your doctor. Sometimes it is a physical problem (artery disease; diabetes).

Painful intercourse (dysparevnia) in a woman can be emotionally or physically determined. Medical advice is needed if this is a recurring problem.

With advancing years, the male erection may be less easily aroused and less firm. A woman's lubricant glands may be less active. These are normal, common events. Prescription: Take two people in the mood; add a little baby oil, and a little imagination.

To quote the same Irishman as before, "May you live as long as you want to, and may you want to as long as you live."

c. ENTER THE DOCTOR

After 65, medical needs begin to increase. Older people see a doctor more often than younger people. More seniors are admitted to hospital. Self-responsibility is very important in maintaining good health, but you do need to have a good doctor.

Don't wait until you need a doctor before finding one. Everyone needs a periodic checkup. Certain examinations should be carried out at regular intervals, especially as you get into late middle age. Blood pressure should be checked annually even in the most healthy. Breast and pelvic examinations are advised for women on a regular basis.

A good family doctor will co-ordinate your needs for checkups, and is available as a counsellor on health maintenance. Even if you are disgustingly healthy, you should see a family doctor periodically. If you get sick, you then have a doctor who knows you! If you need a specialist and hospital care, you have a friend who can navigate the sometimes confusing path among several specialists in a big hospital. Your doctor is responsible for you and to you.

Finding a good doctor is sometimes time-consuming. Look for a doctor whom you trust (and hopefully like). If you feel that you are "rushed through," and no attention is paid to reasonable questions and requests for explanations, then you have the freedom to choose another doctor. Ask your friends' opinions. Your local medical society will give you doctors' names. Your hospital will have a list of doctors who are taking new patients.

1. Illness

When illness hits you, call your doctor. Reporting early symptoms will enhance better treatment. Don't ignore a new, significant pain and hope it will go away. Don't fail to tell your doctor about a bad dizzy spell, some blood in the urine, or any other unusual event. Don't diagnose yourself! That is your doctor's job.

Common illnesses occur most frequently. Good treatment is available for most of these conditions. If you have coughed up a bit of blood, the odds are that you have bronchitis. This is easily treated. Probably you don't have lung cancer or Chinese lung fluke infestation or some other bad disease. Fear of the worst makes some people stay away from the doctor.

Most fear that we experience is fear of the unknown. We human beings are a pretty tough lot and can face a lot of hard news without falling apart. We can accept a known illness with courage and fortitude. Panic comes in when symptoms remain undiagnosed and our imaginations go wild.

2. Drugs and medicines

"Self help" is quite acceptable if you are dealing with known minor conditions. I want to make a few points about prescription drugs. "Over the counter" medicines are generally pretty safe.

Prescription drugs are all potent and have a definite action on the body. Many have side effects even at the usual doses. You must obey some common-sense rules:

(a) Alcohol and drugs don't mix. Don't drink when you are taking any prescription drug.

(b) Make sure you clearly understand how many pills per day you should take. Don't change the dose without talking to your doctor.

(c) Ask your doctor about possible side effects. (You should be told this anyway.) If side effects occur, report them immediately.

(d) If you are a "doctor-hopper" (a most unwise practice) don't take two or three different drugs from two or three doctors.

It is amazing to me that some folks will visit two doctors for the same illness. Neither doctor knows this is happening. The two prescriptions are taken to different drug stores. What usually happens is that double doses of the same drug are taken. This is the road to disaster! You are certainly entitled to a second opinion about diagnosis and treatment. But don't confuse this basic right with "doctor-hopping."

(e) Sleeping pills and tranquilizers have their place in treatment; however, some doctors prescribe them for too long. Some patients demand them. I have lost many patients over the years because I wouldn't be a "good guy" and give a prescription for one of these drugs. It is reasonable to prescribe these drugs in many instances. However, it is not reasonable in many cases for a person to be "on a tranquilizer" for years just because they "feel better."

3. Doctor-patient problems

Many complaints are heard about doctors. Many are directed to medical societies. Sometimes lawyers are retained. In the majority of cases, the patient has never voiced the complaint to the doctor! Talk to the doctor first (not the secretary). If not satisfied, then of course, carry your complaint further.

Many complaints are due to lack of communication. Doctors and patients both have to improve these lines of communication. We are, after all, both trying for the same goal — to maintain your health or get you over an illness.

4. Conclusions

You as a patient have to take responsibility for your own health. A good doctor-patient relationship will enhance the quality of health care you receive.

17
MAKING YOUR FINAL PLAN

a. SET YOUR GOALS

Up to this point you have been examining parts of your life as if they were separate entities, but life is complex and consists of many parts and to work satisfactorily the parts must fit together to make a functioning unit. Now is the time to do this, to bring them together to plan a full, rounded, and satisfying life.

Success is most likely if there is a plan. Therefore, first decide what you really want in your retirement and then make a plan to achieve it. This is a very personal thing, no one else can know what is important or irrelevant to you. Decide what you would like to do or achieve, include your fantasies for they may not be as far-fetched as you fear, and only eliminate them later if they are crowded out or deemed not worth the cost. If equipment or training is required, set up a timetable for each phase to be sure it will be done. If this is to be a really different stage of life, doing those things that were deferred for practical reasons will make it so.

Life is what you do as time passes; how you use that procession of moments determines how it can be evaluated. Therefore, begin your planning by thinking out how your time can be best spent. What will you do with the days so that at the end of each there will be a feeling of contentment? It need not all be classed as fun; part must be used for the requirements of living.

Your activities may be different from those of younger years, but so are your needs and goals. Change is not new with retirement, but has occurred with every stage of your life since birth.

Retirement is like turning off a crowded, high-speed freeway onto an unpaved country road. No longer must you strain to keep your place and watch the traffic. The tension fades away, you slow down. There is still much time, but it is not endless. Many avenues are now closed, but many new ones are opened. Your days are now entirely at your disposal.

b. THE NEW VALUE OF TIME

Time takes on a new value. During working years it was sold for the money to buy the necessities of life and its purchaser was often a hard task master who demanded full value. Now it takes on a new dimension — it has become the coin used to buy your pleasures and satisfactions because it is no longer needed to buy the goods and services. The means to purchase necessities was stored away over the years as pay deductions or savings and now return as pension and investment income.

A new supply of time comes each day. It differs from money in that it cannot be stored but melts away like ice in the summer sun and if not spent upon arrival is lost forever. Could there be a more shameful waste than to permit life to melt away unused?

c. DO NOT BELIEVE IT!

There are many unfounded myths related to aging, and to accept them could be a barrier to planning the best kind of life that is possible.

The first is that it is difficult to learn new things. How this arose no one knows, but ability in this respect is probably related to one's desires or attitude. If you want to learn, you can; it has been proven that the capability to do so remains as good as ever well into advanced age. Because of a wealth of experience, it may be possible for the older person to see concepts more readily and absorb them more quickly than when they were younger.

There is the problem of forgetfulness, which is really a slowness rather than an inability, for there is so much stored in the mind at this stage that it may take longer to sort through and recall the desired information. However, it seems to come back as well as ever after a short interval.

d. BE ACTIVE

Physical strength and energy does decline and it will impose restrictions. These are not as serious as in the past for there are so many mechanical aids to take the place of muscle: golf carts, ski lifts, the automobile, outboard motors, power lawn mowers, elevators, and all sorts of specialized equipment. Living accommodation on one floor or reached by elevators eliminates climbing stairs.

Have you noticed how few crippled people there are compared to the number around when you were young? Medical care has prolonged good health and new surgical procedures revitalize many. As an example, that old crippler, the painful, worn out hip joint is now often completely replaced, which permits painless, normal movement.

Many people in the past suffered from what was frequently diagnosed as senility, but was simply a turning inward usually caused by living alone and losing touch with others and the world around them. Now that this is understood, it can be prevented by proper lifestyle, and often those who are in this position can be brought out of it by bringing them back into a suitable environment. People can remain normal into advanced old age.

e. LOVE CONTINUES

In past generations love and sex were never discussed publicly or in the media. There was much ignorance and misunderstanding, and it was feared that sexual activity would terminate at a relatively early age. Now these things are being investigated by qualified people and their findings publicized and more fully discussed. The indications are that sexual activity can continue into old age, probably at a reduced level, but still with as great a meaning and importance to human relationships as ever. A mutually satisfying love life can continue indefinitely if the partners wish it.

f. A LIFE WITH QUALITY

While some pleasures may be ruled out on the grounds of physical requirements, many others are available to replace them. It is foolish to feel that there is nothing left if certain cherished pastimes must end, for there are so many others to replace them that the prospect for enjoyment remains. There is the time to try, to sort out, and to choose. There are so many prospects and so many people available to help, and so many organizations offering special discounts, rights, and opportunities for the retired that everyone has the possibility of having a satisfying and rewarding life. It is, however, another example of taking the horse to water — the horse must drink, you cannot do it for it. Likewise, you must make the decisions and the effort yourself to grasp the opportunities.

No previous retiring generation has had the opportunity which is before you. On average, you are retiring while physically active and at an earlier age. You can look forward to a longer life span in better health and with greater financial security. You have handled more difficult periods in life than this — take advantage of this opportunity which you and your fellow Canadians have prepared.

APPENDIX 1
CHECKLIST FOR RETIRING

Prior preparation

1. Think about retirement and the changes it will bring.

2. Prepare your retirement life plan with your spouse if you have one.

3. Obtain all details respecting pensions and insurances (group, life, income maintenance, health and disability policies) offered through group plans at your place of employment. Know the benefits you are entitled to while employed there and the options open to you on leaving or retiring.

4. Examine details of personally owned life insurance, pension plans, or registered retirement savings programs. Consider changes as suggested in chapter 10. Do not delay finding these facts until retirement. They should be part of planning all your personal programs.

5. Estimate financial position in retirement and work toward any changes desired to increase income and/or decrease expenses.

6. Obtain birth or baptismal certificate if you do not have one.

7. Obtain card from Canada Pension Plan office and mail to Ottawa for a record of payments. Discuss with counsellor at Income Security office to determine size of pension.

8. When one spouse has reached 65 and the other 60, consider the possibility of applying for a Spouse's Allowance.

9. Apply for Canada Pension three months prior to retirement.

One year prior to retirement

10. Discuss with employer his or her policy respecting retirement, options for continued employment, and all benefits and options you may have.

Six months prior to 65th birthday

11. Apply for Old Age Security Pension and for Canada Pension.

On 65th birthday

12. If your income is below a minimum you may be eligible for Guaranteed Income Supplement (GIS).

On retirement

13. Meet with responsible officer at place of employment. Discuss again all benefits to which you are entitled. Be sure to get wages, holiday pay, and any cash coming from company benefit plans.

14. Obtain list of any health, medical, and hospital plans that have been paid by employer but which you must now pay directly. Get instructions and forms and apply at once.

15. Obtain a list of any options you have respecting group insurance, pension, etc. Do not decide these in haste. Take information and decide carefully at home after receiving any advice you desire.

16. Have medical and dental examinations.

17. Both you and your spouse make or review wills.

18. Start quarterly income tax payments if necessary.

APPENDIX 2
HEALTH CARE IN CANADA

The Canada Health Act is a federal law that sets the minimum requirements for hospital and medical care in Canada. Under it, each province has an insurance plan that will pay for all the designated services to its members. It is financed partially by federal grants and the remainder by premiums charged to the members and/or general provincial funds.

Each province sets the fees it pays for care, charging the patient extra for the designated services that are not covered.

The premium charged is set by each province, but there is no charge for a single person 65 or over, or for a couple when one spouse reaches 65. Most prescription drugs are paid for by the plan.

A charge may be permitted for non-designated services such as an examination for insurance or other non-essential services. Many physicians do not make these charges; most will not if the patient objects, particularly on the grounds of inability to pay.

New Brunswick permits doctors to opt out of their plan for certain services and, provided the patient agrees, the doctor can charge directly but the patient is not reimbursed by the plan. The New Brunswick Medical Society has guaranteed to provide insured service if requested so that no one is forced to pay unwillingly.

Each province also sets its own rules describing out-of-province coverage for the insured. If you are going to visit or move out of province, look into the details of your plan.

Everyone should get a copy of their provincial plan and become familiar with what is and is not covered and the premium applicable.

APPENDIX 3
CANADIAN VOLUNTEER CENTRES

If the provincial address shown is not near your home, contact the one in your province and request the location of the nearest centre.

Alberta

Volunteer Centre of Calgary
1129-17 Avenue S.W.
Calgary T2I 0B6

Volunteer Action Centre
9844-110 Street
Edmonton T5K 1J2

British Columbia

Volunteer Centre
1625 West 8th Avenue
Vancouver V6J 1T9

Manitoba

Volunteer Centre of Winnipeg
311-267 Edmonton Street
Winnipeg R3C 1S1

New Brunswick

Volunteer Centre
P.O. Box 7091, Station A
Saint John E2L 4S5

Moncton Volunteer Centre de Benevolat
68 Highfield Street
Moncton E1C 5N3

The Volunteer Bureau of Fredericton
300 St. Mary's Street
Fredericton E3A 2S4

Bathurst Volunteer Centre
1917 Vallee Lourde
R.R. #3, Suite 3
Box 30
Bathurst E2A 4G8

Newfoundland

Community Services Council
P.O. Box 5116
St. John's A1C 5V3

Nova Scotia

Volunteer Centre
P.O. Box 329
Pugwash B0K 1L0

Volunteer Bureau Help Line
c/o Dalhousie University
Coburg Road at Oxford Street
Halifax B3H 3J5

Ontario

Senior V.I.P. Services
Volunteer Service of Metro Toronto
344 Bloor Street W.
Toronto M5S 1W9

Prince Edward Island

Voluntary Resource Council
218 Kent Street
Charlottetown C1A 1P2

Quebec

Service Benevole de Montreal
12466 Bishop Street
Montreal H3G 2V1

Centre d'Action benevole
180 Ville Vanier
Quebec City G1S 2V1

Saskatchewan

Volunteer Bureau of Regina
2231 Broad Street
Regina S4P 1Y7

OTHER TITLES IN THE SELF-COUNSEL RETIREMENT SERIES

MARGO OLIVER'S COOKBOOK FOR SENIORS
Nutritious recipes for one — two — or more
by Margo Oliver

Cooking expert Margo Oliver presents appetizing recipes along with useful kitchen know-how in this book designed especially for seniors. In her personal style, she addresses some of the special concerns of mature adults while keeping the flavor in the food.

Whether you are a novice or experienced cook, whether you are cooking for yourself or more, you'll find these recipes — over 150 — interesting and fun to make. $9.95

Contents include:

- Kitchen helpers
- Know-how for new cooks
- Appetizers, Snacks, and Sips
- Soups and Sauces
- Main Dishes
- Salads and Vegetables
- Breads and Cereals
- Sweets
- Suggested Menus

WISE AND HEALTHY LIVING
A commonsense approach to aging well
by Richard D. Underwood and
Brenda Breeden Underwood

Retirement years can be full of activity and happy times if approached with a positive attitude and a willingness to make minor changes to adapt to changing physical and psychological needs. This book presents a holistic approach to aging and health. It discusses the aging process and the changes to be expected, how to deal with change, and how it may affect the way you live. $8.95

FIT AFTER FIFTY
Feel better —live longer
by Dr. Roy J. Shephard and Dr. Scott G. Thomas

This book explains the importance of exercise, the effects of aging on how you exercise, how to exercise, precautions to take, special considerations for those with particular health problems, and perhaps most important, the great variety of enjoyable activities that qualify as exercise. $8.95

HOUSING OPTIONS FOR OLDER CANADIANS
Choosing a safe, comfortable, and affordable lifestyle
by Jim Wilson

As you get older, your needs and wants change. You may long for a warmer climate or a smaller yard. Perhaps you want to stay in the home you love but wonder how long you can manage it. Maybe you dream of packing all your belongings into an RV and taking to the road. Or perhaps you are wondering about a new home in a new community.

What are the choices? What are the pros and cons of each one? How do you decide what will be best for you? And when you have made your decision, how will you afford it?

This book describes the options and uses worksheets to help you pinpoint the ones you prefer. $11.95

You will discover —

- How to analyze your location needs

- What kind of housing suits you best

- Whether you are a small-town or big-city person

- The costs and bonuses of moving

- How to modify and maintain your home

- The pros and cons of home-sharing, co-ops, joint ownership, and mobile homes

ORDER FORM

All prices are subject to change without notice. Books are available in book, department, and stationery stores. If you cannot buy the book through a store, please use this order form. (Please print)

Name _____

Address _____

_____

Charge to:
❑Visa   ❑ MasterCard

Account Number _____

Validation Date_____

Expiry Date _____

Signature _____

Please send your order to the nearest location:
Self-Counsel Press, 1481 Charlotte Road
North Vancouver, B. C. V7J 1H1

Self-Counsel Press, 8-2283 Argentia Road
Mississauga, Ontario L5N 5Z2

❑Check here for a free catalogue outlining all of our publications.

Please add $2.68 for postage and handling ($2.50 postage and $.18 GST). Please add GST to your book order.
YES, please send me:

_____copies of **Margo Oliver's Cookbook for Seniors**, $9.95

_____copies of **Wise and Healthy Living**, $8.95

_____copies of **Fit After Fifty**, $8.95

_____copies of **Housing Options for Older Canadians**, $11.95